South American Cooking

Foods and Feasts from the New World

South American Cooking

Barbara Karoff

Illustrated by Earl Thollander

Aris Books

Addison-Wesley Publishing Company, Inc.

Reading, Massachusetts   Menlo Park, California   New York
Don Mills, Ontario   Wokingham, England   Amsterdam   Bonn
Sydney   Singapore   Tokyo   Madrid   San Juan

Many of the designations used by manufacturers and sellers to distinguish their products are claimed as trademarks. Where those designations appear in this book and Addison-Wesley was aware of a trademark claim, the designations have been printed in initial capital letters (e.g., Eagle Brand condensed milk).

Library of Congress Cataloging-in-Publication Data

Karoff, Barbara, date.
    South American cooking : foods and feasts from the New World /
Barbara Karoff.
        p.   cm.
    Bibliography: p.
    Includes index.
    ISBN 0-201-51799-X (Addison-Wesley)
    ISBN 0-201-55094-6 (pbk.)
    1. Cookery, Latin American.   2. Menus.   I. Title.
TX716.A1K37   1989
    641.598—dc19   89-362
                                                                                 CIP

Aris Books Editorial Offices and Test Kitchen
1621 Fifth Street
Berkeley, CA 94710
(415) 527-5171

Book design by Douglass G. A. Scott
Cover art © by Lisa Tysko
Illustrations © by Earl Thollander

Set in 11 point Bodoni Book by Compset, Inc., Beverly, MA

ABCDEFGHIJ-VB-943210
First printing, August 1989
First paperback printing, August 1990

To David, Paul, John, and Philippe

Contents

List of Recipes by Country

Chile

Colombia

Acknowledgments

To the many people who contributed their time and talents to this book, I sincerely thank you all.

And, I offer special thanks to:

Rita Kramer and Jean Smith for introducing me to Delta Lines. Without that introduction, this book would not have happened. The Delta officers and staff in San Francisco and aboard the *Santa Maria* and the *Santa Magdalena*, Second Steward Bill Kaler whose cheerful assistance made my shipboard cooking sessions successful on both voyages, Meredith Pechoultres, Fred Stone, Bill Sistrunk, George Merritt and my mentors aboard the *Santa Maria*, Norma and Warren Boin. Judy McCormick, Maria de la Calle Thorson, and the staff and guests at the Aris kitchens, where every recipe was tested and tasted, for their help with the recipe development. Mimi Luebbermann for her dedicated encouragement in launching this project—I am forever grateful. Frances Bowles for her expert advice and skillful cooperation. My POWW peers Barbara Arnoldussen, Dale Bryant and Millie Edison for their unrelenting support. Finally, I want to thank my agent Martha Casselman, my editor John Harris, and my illustrator Earl Thollander.

I needed each and every one of you. I appreciate your help, your friendship, and your loyalty.

The Santa Maria leaving Rio

Introduction

In 1492 Christopher Columbus sailed to the Americas aboard his good ship the *Santa Maria* on a voyage that changed the world. Almost five hundred years later, I sailed around the South American continent on another *Santa Maria*, on a voyage that changed my world. On that voyage, and on another a year later, I discovered the cuisines of the ten South American countries. I began in earnest to study the history, sociology, and anthropology of the countries that produced them, studies that seemed necessary if I were really to understand and appreciate the diverse and often unfamiliar foods of the continent.

I quickly learned that like most North Americans, even the well traveled, I knew little about South American food. Culturally, historically, and artistically, a good many of our roots are elsewhere and our bond with the southern continent is frequently more one of location than anything else. Partly that is because travel to South America is often complicated and difficult. The continent is so large that most visitors simply fly into and out of the popular cities or stop briefly at the Caribbean and Atlantic ports that until recently were the only ones included in the itineraries of most cruise ships. Happily, the cruise ship schedules are changing to include more of South America.

I have been fortunate to make two trips from San Francisco down the west coast of Mexico and Central America, through the Panama Canal, all the way down the Atlantic coast of South America, through the Strait of Magellan, up the west coast of the continent and back to San Francisco—two two-month odysseys aboard the wonderful although slightly aging, Delta Lines cargo-passenger ships. On both trips I visited Colombia, Venezuela, Brazil, Argentina, Chile, Peru, and Ecuador and on both trips I provided demonstrations for the passengers, of the preparation of South American food. I shared my research on the cuisines and my experiences in the local produce markets and restaurants.

Traveling by ship on a long voyage was a new experience for me and I quickly succumbed to its many pleasures. I loved the leisurely pace and the wonderful gift of time and, after long, lazy days at sea, I never tired of observing the slow, quiet approaches to port and all the tasks and rituals of our arrivals and departures.

Before my first journey, I read books on South America, travel books, cook books, history books, sociology books, and novels. I studied the art, architecture, and archaeology. I reviewed my trips to Spain and Portugal. I collected South American recipes and tested them. In fact, I cooked South American food almost exclusively for many months. Then, as we circled the continent, I shopped in the colorful, sometimes exotic, food markets. I sampled as much of the local fare as time in port allowed and returned to the ship loaded with weird-looking bundles and bags of wonderful things for "show and tell."

Eating ashore was always a pleasure. I was first dazzled and then delighted by the bounty of tropical fruits, some familiar and some not, presented for dessert after a lovely lunch in Caracas. Even the old favorites tasted more luscious and sweet than they had ever tasted before.

In Buenos Aires I was quickly seduced by the selection of *empanadas* at several small restaurants. They were perfectly seasoned and exceptionally good. The waitress was anxious for me to try each and every variety. She needn't have worried; I wouldn't have done otherwise.

I was fortunate to be in wonderfully exuberant Rio de Janiero on a Saturday afternoon because that is when many restaurants add *Feijoada completa* to their menus. That complex but earthy meal eaten with a crowd of lively *Cariocans* while overlooking the beach at Ipanema, added up to perfect pleasure. Even though the day was tropically warm, the meal was completely right.

The local fish and shellfish in Chile and Peru were always part of the outstanding and beautifully prepared meals both at elegant hotels and simple cafés. When I got to Ecuador, I learned why their *ceviche* is a source of national pride. I had an especially memorable version, bitter with the tang of Seville oranges, at a small open-air café right beside the docks in the busy little port of Manta.

Partly because I am not entirely a purist, but mostly because I want the recipes I have chosen to be used and enjoyed, I have taken a selective approach to the foods of South America. Many ingredients, especially many varieties of the chili peppers, potatoes, corn, and fish that give certain South American dishes their distinctive character, are virtually unavailable even in our best-stocked ethnic markets, so some adaptation is necessary. After studying, cooking, testing, and tasting South American food for a long time, I am convinced that certain dishes will please our North American palates far more than others will. *Yuca*, no matter how it is prepared, guinea pig, numerous overly sweet desserts, and many of the complicated preparations of dried salt cod, I leave to the text-books. A few of the recipes I have chosen are not entirely authentic, but have been included to show how the spirit of South American cuisine may be adapted to other ingredients or styles of cooking.

All the recipes included in this book produce dishes that are good to eat and are well worth trying. I have made every effort to interpret them carefully and fairly. When I have changed a recipe, it has been to make it more practical and attractive and the changes are noted. And, as any good cook knows, recipes are reinterpreted and changed by countless cooks in their native countries every day because such is the fate of well-used and well-loved recipes the world over.

My cooking sessions aboard the *Santa Maria* and the *Santa Magdalena* invariably met with enthusiasm and, on more than one occasion, with surprise at just how good the dishes of South America are. Later, testing and tasting recipes in the Aris Test Kitchen with a more sophisticated group confirmed the results aboard ship. I hope you will agree.

Part I

The Foods of South America

In the market, Santos, Brazil

The Great International Food Exchange

Today's South American food closely reflects the history of the continent. Geographic areas are often more important than the ones described by national boundaries. In very few cases did the colonizers from the Iberian peninsula adapt their cooking and eating styles to those of the local inhabitants. Instead, they changed their life-styles as little as possible by importing familiar foods from their homelands almost immediately. The newcomers did not, however, ignore the wealth of new foods they found in the New World; they simply incorporated them into their own styles of cooking to create, over several generations, today's creole cuisines. The daily fare of the original Indians and their often woefully poor descendants has changed little over the years. Its limited variety makes it of limited interest to us.

To understand the food of South America it helps to know a little history. I've found the subject fascinating and not without a few surprises.

In the sixteenth century, the Conquistadors set out from Spain close on the heels of Columbus and the other great discoverers. *Their* objective was gold. Cortes robbed and overran Montezuma's sophisticated Aztec civilization in 1519 and he was not disappointed. Pizarro was also lucky when he emptied the treasuries of the great Inca Empire fourteen years later. Ironically, the stolen gold and silver contributed little to and had few lasting effects on future generations anywhere. Other discoveries, surprisingly many of them involving food, were to be of far more lasting value and consequence.

Fortunately for us, the Conquistadors and those who followed them were men of curiosity, discoverers and traders as well as harsh conquerors and colonizers. They encountered exotic prepared foods and as yet unknown food crops wherever they ventured. Spanish military expeditions seldom set forth without scientists and clergy in tow and we owe much to those literate few who jotted notes, compiled descriptions, and collected seeds and cuttings as they trudged about in the vast new lands.

The new foods the Spaniards shipped home added considerably and immediately to a great international food exchange that was just beginning to gain momentum. In the sixteenth century the world was circumnavigated for the first time and, as a result, foods were on the move from one continent to another. The adoption, adaptation, and synthesis of these new foods eventually created the national cuisines we know today.

Of course, the mingling began centuries earlier, but one has only to read a list of foods indigenous to the New World to know that the big impetus came with Europe's discovery of the Western Hemisphere less than five hundred years ago. Plant foods native to the Americas have far more effectively altered the course of history and changed people's lives than have all the vast treasures of the Aztecs and the Incas. Even the worldwide population increase that occurred in the late seventeenth century is attributed in part to the availability of new foods from the New World.

The cuisines of present-day Mexico are not included in this book, but the indigenous plant foods of Mexico, and in some cases, of Central America and the Caribbean Islands as well, must be included. The Spanish discoveries are better documented in Mexico than they are elsewhere, thanks mostly to the fascinating accounts of Bernardo de Sahagun, a Spanish friar who wrote about his experiences soon after the conquest, and of Bernal Díaz del Castillo, a soldier in Cortes's company, who penned his remarkably fresh and detailed recollections fifty years later.

Although no contact among the three great Latin American Indian civilizations has been documented, the Mayas, Aztecs, and Incas each depended on corn, the continent's only native grain, for their survival. Once they became settled, the early Indians also cultivated beans and squash. All three crops were unknown in the outside world, but they became the staple trio of the South American diet at an early date and, despite the many more sophisticated foods available today, this durable triad still dominates the diets of many South Americans.

Although the fruits of most wild plants in the early stages of evolution are insignificant, small, and not particularly tasty, the early Indians in choosing corn, beans, and squash, made wise choices. Each is easy to grow and store but they have other advantages—more esoteric, no less practical, and far more interesting.

To label the pre-Aztec and pre-Inca farmers budding horticulturists may overstate their skills, but they did choose three plant foods that naturally complement one another. Beans enrich the soil for both corn and squash and replenish the nitrogen that corn takes from it. Corn is deficient in the amino acid lysine, so that its protein is unusable by the human body. But, combined in the diet with lysine-rich and therefore nutritionally compatible beans, the corn protein becomes available. The lush foliage of the squash plants contributes by conserving moisture in the soil.

The potato, better adapted than is corn to the high altitudes where the Inca empire flourished, has been the staple crop of the Andean Indians since prehistoric times. In fact, the tiny, rock-hard, freeze-dried potatoes found at pre-Inca grave sites, antedate by centuries today's high-tech, dried trail food. Many of the ancient Andean terraces, engineering marvels built by a people who had not developed the wheel and who did not have strong draft animals, are still in use today. Slopes of forty-five degrees terraced for a thousand feet above the valley floors are not uncommon. Potatoes are still cultivated up to elevations of fourteen thousand feet in parts of Peru, Ecuador, Bolivia, Chile, and Argentina. In Peru more than one hundred varieties are grown today, many of them all but unknown outside the mountain regions of the Andes. The Aztecs, who enjoyed an easier life in their fertile Mexican valley, knew nothing of the potato and even today it is not an important food in Mexico. Nor was it an instant success when it was introduced to Europe soon after the Conquest. Its value and importance today far exceed that of the plundered Inca treasury. Pizarro would be surprised by this, no doubt, and probably bewildered as well.

The early explorers found many more new foods than corn, beans, squash, and potatoes. The Western Hemisphere was lacking in domesticated animals but it was not lacking in domesticated and potentially domesticable plant foods, foods so wide-ranging, in fact, that it is difficult to think of a cuisine anywhere in the world today that has not benefited and been changed by the discoveries in the New World. Our own eating habits would be quite different without Latin America's bounty which, from the immensely important to the merely delightful or interesting, includes: allspice, arrowroot, avocados, beans, Brazil nuts, cashew nuts, chili peppers, chocolate, corn, guavas, *jicama*, manioc, nasturtiums, papayas, passion fruit, peanuts, pineapples, potatoes, squash, tomatoes, turkeys, and vanilla.

Some of the foods on this impressive list are very old indeed. Avocado seeds dating from 8000 B.C. have been found in Mexico and the Aztecs and the Incas both maintained large avocado orchards at the time of the Conquest. Beans, along with corn, are still the most widely eaten food in South America and are consumed with pleasure each day by people of all classes. They, too, are an ancient food. Archaeologists have found them at Cache civilization sites, a culture established in the Peruvian Andes about 2700 B.C. By between 1700 and 1800 B.C., lima beans were being grown on the coast of what is now Peru. Of course, they weren't called lima beans then because the name came later—after Pizarro laid out the city that is the capital of Peru today.

Brazil nuts have also been around a long time and were growing in the Amazon valleys of Brazil long before the Portuguese or the Spanish arrived. Cashew nuts, too, were under cultivation when the Europeans appeared. The *chayote* squash dates back to the Aztecs who called it *chayotl*; it is still an important South American vegetable.

After defeating Montezuma and destroying his grand capital, Cortes and his surviving followers stopped briefly at the old Mayan city of Chichén Itzá to shop for seeds and plants and included on their shopping list were cacao beans. Cortes was probably the first European to taste chocolate and he had not forgotten the frothy drink he savored at Montezuma's table.

Manioc, or bitter cassava, is a food almost unknown in North America and Europe (and, in my opinion, likely to remain so) but in South America and West Africa it is consumed daily in some form by 250 million people. Along with corn, sweet potatoes, and peanuts, manioc traveled from South America to West Africa with the Europeans. How the primitive Indians learned the complex process of removing the cyanide from the tubers remains a mystery.

Protein-rich peanuts have been known in South America since at least pre-Inca times. Recent finds in China may prove that the little legume developed there independently or the discoveries may indicate some contact between China and the Western Hemisphere in the second millennium B.C. For now, however, South America still gets credit as the original habitat. Whatever is eventually decided about their origin, it is known that they traveled with the Portuguese and Spanish from South America to become an important food crop in Africa. The peanut-rich sauces and stews of West Africa, the Bahia region of Brazil, and the highlands of Peru and Ecuador have much in common.

Most of the pineapples we eat in the United States today are flown in from Hawaii, but the fruit is native to tropical South America. Along with the papaya and the sweet potato, it was introduced into Asia and the Pacific islands about a hundred years after Columbus's voyages.

Some varieties of squash were known in South America as far back as the Cache civilization in the Andes and were cultivated on the Peruvian coast by 1800 B.C. Easily grown, as most varieties are, they quickly became established in their new environments and later traveled throughout the world. In many cultures, the fruit and the flower, which are often on the vines at the same time, represent fertility.

Sweet potatoes, unlike white potatoes, were an immediate hit wherever they were introduced. They preceded the whites to Europe, thanks to Columbus, and journeyed from South America to China about a hundred years later.

Tomatoes were another of Cortes's discoveries in the Valley of Mexico. It is all but impossible to imagine southern European, Middle Eastern, or Mediterranean cuisines today without the tomato, so ubiquitous it has become, but again, acceptance took time.

Another product of Mexico's fertile land, vanilla, was used and enjoyed by the sophisticated Montezuma and appreciated by Bernardo de Sahagun who told his European readers how the Aztecs combined chocolate and vanilla to create a memorable after-dinner drink.

These were the more important foods that traveled to Europe from the New World, but it was far from a one-way affair. The colonizing Portuguese and Spanish were quick to bring their own foods and animals to the New World and the Iberian peninsula offered its bounty generously. As always, dynamic things happen when one culture is imposed upon or merged with another.

Chickens and pigs were among the first arrivals from the Old World. Rats and cats, who escaped from ships, also settled in early. Balboa landed fierce dogs which he intended to turn on the Indians, but the clever natives tamed the dogs and turned them into pets.

Garlic and onions—how can we even think of today's South American cooking without them?—were also among the first foods to cross from east to west. They were easily transported and just as easily grown. The clergy specialized in raising and propagating aromatic herbs in their mission gardens. Another early arrival was olive oil. An established necessity in Spanish kitchens, it quickly became important in the new lands where oils and fats were all but unknown. With the arrival of cattle, dairy products were available in the Americas for the first time.

Colonial diets were soon supplemented by wheat, barley, rice, and rye. Rice, which is indigenous to India, had reached Spain and Portugal with the Moors, and eventually became one of the most important foods in South America. Wheat has never displaced corn in South America but, for many Europeans and their creole descendants, it was and is important both as a food and a status symbol.

Garbanzo beans and lentils, both favorites in the Mediterranean world, soon accompanied the Spanish to their new homes and were found to be beautifully compatible with a number of native foods. The accumulations of lentils that I noticed between the cobblestones on the docks of many South American ports are modern testimony to the continuing trade.

Bernal Díaz del Castillo, Cortes's lively chronicler, is credited with taking orange seeds to Mexico in 1518, although Columbus had planted seedlings on several Caribbean islands as early as 1493. Oranges were native to China and had an alternating history of prominence and obscurity before the Moors transformed parts of southern Spain into vast orange groves in the twelfth century. By 1587, orange trees planted by the Portuguese were thriving in Brazil and, today, it is believed that all navel oranges grown in the United States are descended from a pair of trees that once grew in Bahia.

Most authorities agree that sugarcane originated in India and was another of the many foods introduced into Spain and Portugal during the Moorish occupation. The first planting in the New World is again attributed to Columbus who set out cuttings in Cuba during his second voyage. Sugarcane production eventually motivated the Portuguese to import slaves to Brazil when a workforce of 250 laborers was considered necessary to operate even the smallest plantation at a profit. Similarities of climate and geography in north-eastern Brazil and western Africa helped the slaves to flourish despite their status. Today their impact on Brazil's Bahian cuisine is not only unchallenged but lauded.

Okra is one of several foods that traveled west with the slaves from Africa to become popular, not only in Brazil, but later in the southern United States as well.

The coffee plant also arrived in South America from Africa but had nothing to do with the slave trade. After its start in Ethiopia, it made its way to Europe via the Middle East and in the eighteenth century was transported to the Caribbean. Today, coffee is firmly established in South America, not only as an export crop, but also as a dearly loved and much consumed beverage.

The conquest of the New World was part of the great age of discovery and exploration that took place all over the world in the sixteenth century. Everywhere, food and plants, as well as people, were on the move. One observing wag described an early sailing ship as looking less like a ship and more like a traveling forest so laden were its decks with flourishing plants!

The mango arrived from India with the Portuguese. Bananas and plantains, also from India and Malaysia, arrived in the New World via Africa and the Canary Islands. In 1516 Tomás de Berlanga, a Spanish friar, took a rhizome of the plant to the Americas and today, Colombia and Ecuador are among the world's leading banana producers.

The chili pepper, one of Latin America's greatest culinary gifts to the world, is so important and the varieties so numerous that I have set aside an entire chapter for them.

Most of the foods introduced into South America by Europeans or Africans still flourish there and later migrations from all over the world have added to the international mix that characterizes the creole cuisines today. Innumerable foods and recipes have been accepted, adapted, refined, and in many cases made distinctively South American by talented local cooks. In ever more refined ways, the great food exchange continues today. Whole new crops are seldom introduced from one continent to another anymore, but recipes and methods of preparing food continue to travel and to give pleasure from one continent to another, from one kitchen to another.

Glossary of South American Foods and Ingredients

Many of the so-called exotic ingredients used in South American cooking are becoming increasingly common in our North American grocery and produce stores. Unusual fruits, vegetables, and chilies now fill bins in well-stocked supermarkets and they and other ingredients are available in our Latin, Oriental, and other ethnic markets. We owe the availability of these products in large part to the recent migrations from south of the border and to the continued interest in the cuisine of our own Southwest. A few South American ingredients called for in recipes may be difficult or as yet impossible to obtain here. Substitutions are indicated. The widespread European influences on South American cuisines ensure that most ingredients are as available here as they are there. We will probably never see potatoes and corn in the variety they are found in South American markets but the differences that those omissions make in our cooking will be in degree, not kind.

Not all the foodstuffs that contribute to the distinctiveness of the South American cuisines are exotic. It is often the ways that the foods are used and the combinations that make the resulting dishes interesting and unusual to us. This glossary includes notes on ingredients and their uses. It also includes recipes for coconut milk, chili pepper paste, and paprika-seasoned oil, which are components of dishes rather than dishes themselves.

Annatto (*achiote* in Spanish). The so-called seeds are actually the hard, dry pulp surrounding the seeds of a small flowering tree native to the New World. They are used primarily to make *annatto* oil (*aceite de achiote*), which adds a reddish-orange color and a delicate flavor to a number of South American dishes. Easily prepared, it keeps well in the refrigerator.

**Annatto Oil
(Aceite de achiote)**

4 tablespoons *annatto* seeds

¼ to ½ cup oil or lard

Combine the *annatto* seeds and the oil in a small saucepan and cook slowly over medium heat until the oil becomes orangey-red. Remove from the heat and allow to cool. Strain the oil into a jar that has an airtight lid and refrigerate. The flavor will dissipate if the oil is kept beyond several months.

Added or omitted, *annatto* oil makes little difference to the taste of the finished dish, but don't strive for greater effect by adding seeds directly; they don't soften up even with long cooking. *Annatto* is sold in specialty stores and Latin markets as seeds as well as in powder and paste form. *Annatto* paste, because it includes other seasonings, usually oregano, cumin, black pepper, garlic, and vinegar, should be added to recipes with care. Montezuma's cooks are said to have added *annatto* to chocolate drinks to give them a richer color.

Avocados (Spanish, aguacate; Portuguese, abacate; alligator pear; midshipmen's butter—and many more) are a wonderful food that we do not use with the skill and imagination of South American cooks. We are, however, a step or two more adventurous than the British, who were advised, in an English cookbook published in 1980 "*always* [to] eat avocados raw as an appetizer or in salads." (The emphasis is mine.)

Avocados are ancient. In Peru seeds have been found dating to 2000 B.C. and, in Mexico, dating to 8000 B.C. At the time of the Conquest, the Incas and the Aztecs both had large areas under cultivation. Cortes introduced them to the rest of the world. The Spanish and Portuguese names are corruptions of the Aztec (Nahuatl) *ahuacatl*, which may be translated as "fruit of the testicle tree." The avocado's shape and the fact that it often grows in pairs endowed it very early with supposedly aphrodisiac qualities.

Although there is no proof for this particular sexual fantasy, the avocado does earn high marks for being low in sodium and for containing no cholesterol. It adds both protein and a highly digestible oil to the meatless diets of many South Americans. The avocado is a member of the laurel family and in South America the toasted leaves of the tree are frequently added to the cooking pot in much the same way we use bay (laurel) leaves. The flavor is delightful, but not the same. (To prepare the leaves for cooking, place them in an ungreased iron skillet and toast them over medium heat for about one minute.)

Although there are hundreds of varieties of avocado, only five or six are grown commercially in the United States. The most common varieties are the Hass, in season from April to October, and the Fuerte, available from November to April. The dark, pebbly-skinned Hass turns almost black when it is ripe and is by far the most flavorful.

Avocados darken when the cut surface is exposed to air and drizzling them with lemon or lime juice is never entirely successful. A quicker, easier, and far more reliable solution is simply to rinse all the cut surfaces under cold, running water. There is no added flavor and it works.

Bananas (plátanos in Spanish; bananas in Portuguese), although considered a staple food in the tropics the world over, are not indigenous to tropical South America. They originated in India and in Malaysia and traveled from there to Africa and the Canary Islands. From these sixteenth-century trading centers, the Portuguese and the Spanish took them to the New World. Latin American markets today are known for their prodigious selection, a variety of sizes and colors far beyond the familiar green to yellow fruit of our supermarkets. Some varieties require cooking to make them edible and South Americans, especially the African cooks of Bahia, do this with ingenuity and creativity.

Bananas are available year-round and, although they are among the few fruits that must ripen *off* the tree, they must also be shipped under tightly controlled conditions. They are accommodatingly low in sodium and fat, high in potassium and contain no cholesterol.

Beans (frijoles in Spanish; feijãos in Portuguese), which are native to South America, have been found in Peruvian graves dating back to 3800 B.C. It is beans that helped the great South American food triad, corn, squash and beans to exist by putting a nitrogen-fixing bacteria into the soil to enrich it and make it possible for healthy corn and squash to grow over a period of time.

In Brazil where beans, rice, and manioc are the staff of life, beans provide the protein. The most common beans used in South American cuisines are black, pea, kidney, pinto, and cranberry. Fresh shell beans are also sold seasonally in South America but the types available there are seldom seen in our markets.

Brazil nuts (castanha do pará in Portuguese; castaña de pava in Spanish) really do come from Brazil, from jungle trees that are one hundred thirty feet high, or more and have their lowest branches often a hundred feet off the ground. The nuts in their triangular shells grow, a dozen or so packed together, in a hard, round case, so hard that it takes a sledgehammer to crack it open. The nut meats have a high oil content and are flavorful additions to cakes and confections.

Capsicum—see Chili Pepper Primer page 27.

Cashew nuts (Spanish, anacardos; Portuguese, caju) in the second of their three shells, contain a toxic oil that must be removed by roasting before the nuts are edible and that is probably why most of us have never seen a cashew nut in the shell. The nut is actually the seed of an applelike fruit and is attached, as a small pod or protrusion, at the end and on the outside of the fleshy fruit. Cashews are native to Brazil and contain twenty percent protein.

Cassava is a starchy root vegetable. The whole business of manioc and cassava becomes confusing because so many names come up. Basically, there are two types: sweet cassava and bitter cassava. The root has been a staple in South America for a long time. There is archaeological evidence of its being used as a food as early as 2000 B.C. in the basin of the Amazon and Orinoco rivers. By 1000 B.C., sweet cassava had traveled as far as the coast of Peru. Today, the vegetable is eaten by 250 million people, mostly in South America and West Africa.

Sweet cassava, called *yuca* in the Spanish-speaking countries, and *aipím* in Brazil, is not toxic. It is cooked and eaten in many of the same ways that potato is used and is available, fresh or frozen, in our Latin markets.

Bitter cassava, also called manioc, is a dry starchy tuber that is very low in protein. The root contains cyanide and is highly toxic until it has been extensively processed. Once the toxin is removed, the root is cooked, ground, and processed into flour, called *farinha de mandioca* in Brazil and *fariña* in the rest of South America. When the flour is processed further into pellets, it becomes tapioca, another starchy element in the diet and a product familiar to most North Americans. The stock in which the tuber is cooked is used in soups and the leaves are eaten as a vegetable. The Indians even make a primitive beer from parts of the plant. Mature tubers can remain in the ground for up to two years, a neat solution to the storage problem.

When toasted, manioc (bitter cassava) meal is known as *farofa* and is as common as pepper and salt on Brazilian tables. Variations of *farofa* have become associated with certain dishes, such as the Bahian specialties, *vatapá*, *xin-xim*, and *moqueca*, and the Brazilian national dish, *Feijoada completa*.

Chayote (chu chu, cho cho or, in Brazil, xu xu) is a member of the squash and cucumber family and a native of Central America. The Indians, who called it *chayotl*, were cultivating it when Cortes arrived. It is increasingly available in our markets although we would probably pass it right by if we had only the description of the sixteenth-century Spanish chronicler, Francisco Hernandez, to go by. This gentleman, physician and historian to the court of Philip II, thought it looked "like a hedge-hog"—a more apt description of the jackfruit (see page 19). The *chayote* is similar in size and shape to a pear and ranges in color from dark green to almost white. Because they are bland, they lend themselves to a variety of treatments, but are most often cooked in the same ways as summer squash.

chayote

Cheese (queso in Spanish; queijo in Portuguese). South Americans make a number of local cheeses that are not exported to this country. They also make their own very good versions of Old World cheeses.

Münster Cheese is a particular South American favorite frequently used in cooking. A mild, soft cheese that melts nicely, it was originally (and still is) made in Germany and in the Alsace region of France.

Queso blanco and queso fresco are popular cheeses produced in most of the countries south of the Rio Grande. Both are available here in Latin markets. *Queso blanco* (white cheese) is similar in taste and texture to Münster or mozzarella. Lightly salted, it is made from partly skimmed cow's milk. *Queso fresco* (fresh cheese) is similar in texture to *feta* cheese but less salty. Somewhat crumbly, it is, as the name implies, fresh tasting.

½ cup dried *hontaka* chilies, tightly packed

1 ½ cups boiling water

1 clove garlic

Pinch salt

½ cup boiling chicken stock

3 tablespoons olive oil

Chili Pepper Paste, made with readily available dried *hontaka* chilies, keeps for several weeks if refrigerated in an airtight container and is useful to have on hand if fresh chilies are not available. Substitute 1 teaspoon of this paste for one fresh chili in a recipe.

Break open the dried chilies, and shake out and discard the seeds. Place the chilies in a bowl, cover with the boiling water, and allow them to soak for several hours.

Drain and purée with the remaining ingredients in a blender or food processor to form a smooth paste. Cover tightly and refrigerate. Yields approximately 1 cup.

Choclo is the name given to the small pieces of corn-on-the-cob that are often added to soups and stews in the Spanish-speaking countries or, especially in Peru, that are used to garnish prepared dishes. The word *choclo* also frequently indicates that corn, either on or off the cob, is included in a dish.

Chocolate was popular with the Aztec men (women were not permitted to drink it), who called it *cacauatl*. Although archaeologists believe it was growing in Brazil, in the basin of the Amazon and Orinoco rivers at least four thousand years ago, it was unknown to the then-civilized world until Cortes and his officers dined with Montezuma in 1519. They were enchanted with the exotic beverage—and with the golden goblets in which it was served. They took cacao beans back to Spain where the secrets of chocolate making were guarded closely for almost one hundred years.

When the complex process of turning the beans into chocolate finally spread through Europe in the early seventeenth century, the exotic drink was (of course) regarded as an aphrodisiac, a prolonger of life, and a cure for numerous ailments.

Cacao trees grow well commercially only within twenty degrees of the Equator. Ecuador, Venezuela, and Colombia are all producers, but most of the South American harvest comes from Brazil and ninety-five percent of that is produced in the state of Bahia.

Chuño (dried vegetables) may surprise backpackers and wilderness buffs because it proves that the art of freeze-drying food was not only invented in the Andes, but probably in pre-Inca times. The method is used for various tubers that grow at high altitudes, but by far most commonly for potatoes. Once dehydrated, whatever was dried was called *chuño* or *chuñu*. Because *chuño* lasts indefinitely (very ancient specimens have been found in tombs), the Incas kept stores on hand as protection against famine. In the cold Andean highlands, potatoes were allowed to freeze at night. During the day they thawed and were squeezed dry. Again, they froze at night and the process was repeated until the tubers became shrunken, rock-hard, and almost pure starch. Sometimes potatoes were cut up and cooked first and then freeze-dried. Even today, Andean Indians preserve a variety of vegetables by this ancient method.

Cilantro is the Spanish name for the pungent, leafy herb that is also known as fresh coriander or Chinese parsley, depending on the cuisine with which it is associated. It is an annual member of the carrot family, very ancient, and was introduced into the British Isles by the Romans. It traveled to the New World with the Spanish. Cilantro is also important in Oriental and Indian cuisines and its far-flung territory accounts for its being the world's most consumed herb. The flavor is assertive and intense, for many people an acquired taste, but, once acquired, all but addictive. Cilantro enhances other flavors and adds the final fillip to an enormous number of dishes in the South American repertoire. It keeps well in the refrigerator for several days if the stems are submerged in a glass of water and the whole covered loosely with a plastic bag. Growing it at home is less than satisfactory because it so quickly goes to seed.

Coconuts (cocos) were used as food and drink by the Indians in pre-Conquest South America but it was not until the slaves arrived in Brazil that they became important. Authentic Bahian cooking is impossible without coconuts and coconut milk. Fresh coconuts keep about four weeks at room temperature, longer if refrigerated, and the meat freezes beautifully.

The milk, although high in cholesterol, shares many qualities with cow's milk and is a basic cooking liquid in the tropics everywhere.

Coconut Milk (leche de coco; leite de côco) Some recipes call specifically for either thick or thin coconut milk, but most do not. Although acceptable brands are now available in fourteen-ounce cans in Oriental and Latin markets (Chaokoh brand from Thailand is especially good), it is not difficult to make coconut milk at home and, as with all things freshly prepared, there is a difference for the better.

Before purchasing a fresh coconut, give it a good shake to make sure it is full of liquid. That liquid inside is not the milk; it is called coconut water, which it more closely resembles. Once you get the coconut home, take an ice pick or other sharp instrument and pierce two of the three coconut eyes. Then strain the water through a sieve and into a container. Set it aside. Heat the coconut in a 400-degree oven for ten to fifteen minutes. Then wrap it in a dishtowel and crack the shell all over with a hammer. The meat will fall from the shell. If the coconut is to be used only to make coconut milk, do not bother to peel it. If it is destined for other uses, remove the brown skin with a vegetable peeler.

To make thick milk: Place the coconut pieces and 2 tablespoons of the coconut water in a blender or food processor fitted with the steel blade and purée the meat as finely as possible. An average coconut will yield about 4 cups. Put the purée in a fine sieve or in any sieve lined with dampened cheesecloth and pour over it half a cup of hot milk or water. Press to extract as much juice as possible. An average coconut will yield ½ to ¾ cup thick milk.

To make thin milk: Pour up to 3 cups of boiling water (including the reserved coconut water) over the coconut residue left from making the thick milk. Let it stand for 30 minutes and then strain it as for the thick milk. At this point, the coconut meat should be discarded as it has served its purpose.

Unless a recipe specifically calls for thick coconut milk, combine the thick and the thin before using.

Coffee (café) is a major crop and export in Brazil as well as a popular drink with all classes. Over coffee, the country's work is done and the gossip shared. Coffee was first used in Ethiopia. It was taken by Turkish traders to Vienna and from there it traveled to Venice. The Dutch in Surinam (formerly Dutch Guiana) and later the French in French Guiana established the first coffee plantations in the New World and they carefully guarded their secrets for a number of years. The plants were not introduced into Brazil until 1727. Today, most connoisseurs agree that the mountain-grown Colombian beans are superior to those of Brazil but, wherever it is grown, it is consumed and enjoyed all over South America.

1 cup vegetable oil, or half vegetable and half olive oil

2 or 3 cloves garlic, peeled and split in half

3 tablespoons sweet paprika

Color chilena (paprika-seasoned oil) is used liberally in the spicy cuisine of Chile. The ingredients are almost as simple as the name and it keeps indefinitely. An inventive cook will think of uses beyond the Chilean repertoire for this colorful seasoning. I use it to sauté meat, chicken, and fish. Sometimes I drizzle a small amount on hot steamed vegetables and, if I am caught without anything exciting to combine with pasta, I use a small amount of *color* that I warm slightly first.

Place the oil and the garlic in a small ovenproof dish and bake at 350 degrees until the garlic turns brown. Remove the garlic, stir in the paprika; and mix well. When cool, store, tightly covered, in the refrigerator.

Condensed milk is a commercial product not to be confused with, and certainly not interchangeable with, evaporated milk—although both are used extensively in South American cooking. Condensed milk is canned, *contains sugar*, and is very sweet. It is used frequently for desserts, especially in Brazil where they like their sweets very sweet. Condensed milk definitely fills the bill. Borden's Eagle Brand, the only brand I have ever seen in this country, is available in most supermarkets.

Corn—see Maize (page 20).

Custard apple is one of the names of the fruits in the *Annonaceae* family. The number of fruits in the family and the number of names, is confusing but those called the *pawpaw*, *soursop*, and *sweetsop*, are all native to the highlands of Peru and Ecuador and were under cultivation at the time of the Conquest. Common in the Andes today, they come in a number of shapes and sizes, some of which have begun to appear in our better-provisioned markets.

The soursop often grows as large as a watermelon and is also called a *guanábana*. The sweetsop is known in Brazil as *fruta de conde*. All custard apples have a smooth, reddish-brown skin and a sweet, very soft, custardlike flesh. Their flavor has been described as having hints of banana, papaya, and pineapple.

Dendê oil is used in almost every Bahian dish. It adds color, some say texture, and an extremely subtle taste. It is not an essential ingredient although it is easy to find in Latin and specialty food stores. *Dendê* is a type of palm oil, solid, heavy, and a bright fluorescent orange. It arrived in Brazil with the Africans.

Dried salt cod (bacalhau in Brazil; bacalao in the Spanish-speaking countries), is cooked all over South America in what seems to be an endless number of ways. Most of the cod used in South America is imported from Europe where it has long played an important role in Portuguese and Spanish cuisines. In this country it is available at Latin and Oriental markets as well as in some fish markets. Salt cod requires soaking before cooking and, even then, the flavor is stronger than that of fresh fish.

Dried shrimp are important, some say essential, to the Bahian cuisine and for that reason about half of Brazil's huge annual shrimp catch ends up being dried. Scarcely a Bahian dish worth its African heritage does not call for rather large quantities of dried shrimp. These are readily available in Latin and Oriental markets.

Evaporated milk is that familiar supermarket staple we usually call "canned milk." It is unsweetened and not to be confused with condensed milk (see page 17). South Americans use a great deal of it in cooking and, once it is combined with other ingredients, the canned milk taste is seldom identifiable.

Fats and oils were all but unknown in the New World until the Spanish and the Portuguese arrived with cattle and olive oil. Today South American cooks use butter and lard as well as vegetable and olive oil. Unless a distinct flavor of olive oil is desired, any light vegetable oil is appropriate in recipes that call for oil. Butter is frequently chosen for baking although margarine may be substituted.

Feijoda, a fruit unrelated to Brazil's national dish *Feijoada completa*, is a native of Paraguay and Uruguay. Although known as the pineapple guava, it is not a true guava. Recently, it has been cultivated in California so it may soon become more familiar. Its taste is described as a cross between a pineapple and a strawberry.

Garbanzo beans (the Spanish name for chick-peas, and cici and grão-de-bico in Portuguese) date to Neolithic times. They arrived in the New World with the Spanish in the sixteenth century and have been popular there ever since, especially in Brazil and Venezuela.

Ginger (jengibre in Spanish; gengibre in Portuguese) is another of the conquerors' gifts to the conquered. The pungent rhizome fits especially well into the peppery-sweet Bahian cooking where it is firmly entrenched today. Powdered ginger is a poor substitute (some say unacceptable) for the fresh, which is becoming more available in our produce sections.

Jackfruit, also known as *jáca* in Portuguese, are really huge and rather strange looking tropical fruits of the breadfruit genus. They are football-shaped and weigh as much as fifty pounds. A tough, rough, and bumpy green skin protects yellow flesh which is extremely sticky but not particularly tasty.

Jerusalem artichokes (topinambur in Spanish; aleachôfra in Portuguese) are one of the more confusingly named natives of the New World. They are tubers, belong to the sunflower family, and are no relation to the globe artichoke. Nor is there any apparent reason for them to be called Jerusalem. Although a starchy vegetable, they are pleasantly crisp and good either raw or cooked. In our markets they might be called sunchokes or sunroots.

Jícama, a tuber native to Mexico, has recently become popular in parts of the United States. Either raw or cooked, it is crunchy and slightly sweet, a fine substitute for water chestnuts or a crisp addition to a salad or casserole. South of the border, *jícama* is frequently sold on street corners where it is cut into thick fingers, sprinkled with lime juice, salt, and chili powder.

Kale (guita in Spanish; couve in Portuguese) is a primitive form of cabbage, recognizable still from Roman descriptions. Rather than forming a cabbagelike head, its curly leaves grow off a central stalk. Without it, the Brazilian *Feijoada completa* would not be complete and, simply cooked on its own, it is popular as a vegetable in Brazil. Collard greens are quite similar.

Lemons (limón in Spanish; limão in Portuguese) may be either green or yellow in South America. They are a substantial export crop in Chile.

Limes (limas in Spanish; limão-doce in Portuguese) may also be either green or yellow.

Maize (corn—maíz in Spanish; milho in Portuguese) was domesticated seven thousand years ago in Mexico and may have been domesticated independently in Peru at about the same time. It was the most important crop of the Mayas and the Aztecs and, although cultivated in Peru before the potato, it took second place to the tuber in the Inca culture. Today, maize is the most important and most widely cultivated crop in South America.

Prehistoric hunters and gatherers discovered maize in its wild form at a time in its evolution when it was a barely significant food crop. It was, however, adaptable to a variety of geographic conditions and, when domesticated, required less labor than did other basic grains. It was more drought-resistant, easily stored and cooked, and was both durable and portable when dried. And it was nutritious. Today about twenty varieties are grown in the Andes. The Indians recognized its importance and throughout history have endowed maize with supernatural powers. Fossilized ears have been found in ancient Peruvian tombs.

Mangos (mango in Spanish; manga in Portuguese) were grown in India at least four thousand and maybe as many as six thousand years ago, making them one of the world's earliest cultivated fruits. The Portuguese introduced them from India to Europe in the sixteenth century and then brought them on to the New World, some say in exchange for the pineapple. Over one hundred varieties are grown today but, because they are tropical, they remain somewhat exotic to many North Americans. They are, however, eaten by more people in the world than any other fruit.

A really ripe mango is a sweet and luscious treat. They are best when tree-ripened but, as this is not possible for us, they should be kept at room temperature until they ripen. If they have been picked very green and rock hard, they will never ripen well.

Manioc (bitter cassava)—see Cassava, page 12.

Maté or, more properly, yerba maté, is a tealike drink made by steeping the dried leaves of a small holly plant in water. It is slightly bitter, contains a fair amount of caffeine, is mildly stimulating, and is claimed to reduce feelings of fatigue and hunger. It is popular all over South America, but especially so in Brazil, Argentina, Paraguay, Uruguay, and Chile. Latin markets or health food stores sell *maté* loose or in tea bags.

Nasturtiums (capuchina in Spanish; chaga, chagueira, or nastúreo in Portuguese) those bright and pretty garden flowers, are natives of Peru. From there they traveled to Spain and then to France and Flanders. Records in 1597 tell of their shipment from France to England where they are sometimes called Indian cress. Beware of pickled nasturtium seeds masquerading as capers; they are not the real thing. The flowers and leaves are delicate, spicy additions to salads—and wonderfully attractive, too.

Oca is an Andean root vegetable. Although in its native habitat, it is second only to the potato in importance, it is a tuber we are not likely to encounter here.

Okra (quimbombó in Spanish; quiabo in Portuguese), native to Africa and a member of the mallow family, was brought to both North and South America by African slaves. Brazilians, especially in Bahia, use it extensively and imaginatively. It has been endowed with spiritual significance by the voodoo cult of *Candomblé.*

Palm hearts, called palmito in both Spanish and Portuguese, are the tender shoots of a tropical palm tree. In this country they arrive canned from Brazil. In Brazil, they are eaten fresh as well as canned and appear not only as a frequent garnish, but also as appetizers, in soups, salads, and cooked dishes.

Papaya (in Spanish; mamão in Portuguese), another New World native, is sometimes called a tree melon and sometimes (erroneously and in Brazil) a *pawpaw. Pawpaw*, however, is another name for that fruit of many names, the custard apple. Papayas were introduced into Asia about a hundred years after Columbus discovered America and now grow in the tropics all over the world. The unripe fruit contains a useful enzyme called papain that breaks down protein and tenderizes meat. Ripe papayas contain little papain but the fully ripe fruit is a sweet and delicious treat.

Passion fruit (granadilla in Spanish; maracujá-açu in Portuguese) is a native of Brazil and grows well only in subtropical zones. Outward appearances do not win it much acclaim covered as it is with a purplish, leathery, and badly wrinkled skin. The yellow pulp, thick with black seeds, has a tart-sweet flavor that is the very essence of the tropics. The exotic name was given first to the flower rather than to the fruit. According to one story, the early Jesuits saw in the parts of the flower the hammer and nails used in the Crucifixion. Another story says that St. Francis of Assissi saw visions of the passion flower vine growing on the cross.

Passion fruit are beginning to turn up in our markets. They should be stored at room temperature until wrinkly all over but still soft. Then, slit them in half, scoop out the flesh, and eat it with a spoon, seeds and all. Or press the flesh through a sieve and add the purée to fruit salads or desserts. The flavor is assertive and one or two of the small fruit are often enough to achieve the desired hint of the tropics.

Peanuts, those small wonders that have picked up so many names in English, are simply *maní* in South American Spanish or *amendoim* in Portuguese. They are native to South America and have been found at sites in Peru that date from 1800 B.C. Peanuts grow underground and are not real nuts; they are legumes. They contain thirty percent protein and are an important source of that nutrient for many people in South America. Peanut sauces are among the great delights of several South American cuisines.

Pecans are natives to the New World and are related to walnuts. They are, however, seldom used in South American cooking. They are called *pacana* in Spanish.

Pepinos are small roundish melons native to Ecuador where they have grown since pre-Conquest times. Pale yellow with purple stripes, they add a colorful and exotic touch to the fresh produce markets in Peru as well as Ecuador. They are sweet, somewhat bland, and melonlike in taste.

Pineapples (ananás in Spanish; abacaxi in Brazil) got their start in South America and were taken to India possibly in exchange for the mango. What we call *the* pineapple is technically a collection of small fruits: each hexagonal section visible on the outside is botanically an individual fruit. Because they only ripen fully on the plant, pineapples are very perishable in markets and are almost never at their field-ripened best.

Plantains (plátanos in Spanish; banana de saõ-tomé in Portuguese) are more than just big bananas. Although members of the same family, plantains are larger, more starchy, hard to peel and never develop the sweetness and flavor that would make them palatable when raw. They are always eaten cooked and provide a year-round starchy diet for people in tropical zones the world over. Plantains originated in India and Malaysia but had migrated to Africa and the Canary Islands by the sixteenth century. The Spanish and the Portuguese introduced them to South America. Botanically, they are known as *Musa paradisiaca* or fruit of paradise.

Plantain recipes always specify the degree of ripeness required. When green, they contain the most starch and are quite tasteless. At this stage, it is a good idea to peel them under running water to keep the hands from becoming discolored. Experienced cooks often pound green plantains to soften them before cooking. When the fruit turns yellow, it is half ripe and when it turns brown, it is fully ripe. At these two stages, it becomes sweet and the flavor somewhat resembles that of a sweet potato. Black plantains are overripe and taste more like bananas. Cooks in the tropics use plantains in many ways—baked, fried, roasted, boiled and sautéed. Plantains, at whatever stage of ripeness, are not easily peeled and a knife is almost always required.

Potatoes (papas in Spanish; batata in Portuguese) were domesticated in the Andean highlands by the Aymara Indians in pre-Inca times. When they were taken to Europe by Columbus, they were immediately regarded by some as a strong aphrodisiac because they were seen to resemble testicles. The fact that they belong to the nightshade family caused others to believe them poisonous. From this lively and controversial beginning, their path in Europe was anything but smooth, although in South America their acceptance and importance has never waivered.

In South America today a staggering number of varieties of potato are available—well over one hundred, maybe as many as two hundred; the number varies with the source. Some varieties grow only at altitudes above eight thousand feet; some as high as fourteen thousand, but many of the high-altitude crops are bitter and used only for *chuño* (see page 15). Sweet potatoes, the ones that Columbus first took from the New World to the Old, are indigenous to the Amazon River basin and have never encountered an acceptance problem as they traveled around the world.

Prickly pear cactus (nopal in Spanish) are cactus leaves, often referred to as paddles, which have a refreshing, fruity flavor. Latin markets carry them in cans. The fruit is called *tuna*.

South American Pumpkin is zapallo or calabaza in Spanish; abóbora in Portuguese and it's not the same as our pumpkin. In texture it is more spongy and in taste similar to winter squash, which is a good substitute. *Calabaza* is actually a broad term applied to a number of different squash and gourds and frequently refers to the West Indian pumpkin in particular. South Americans use pieces and purées of pumpkin as thickeners in soups and stews. They also cut it into pieces, boil it in syrup, and make it into candy.

Quinces (membrillo in Spanish; manmelo in Portuguese), known in Greek mythology as golden apples, resemble but are not a cross between a pear and an apple. Most often they are made into jam or jelly or into a paste that is served as a dessert. Fruit pastes, an ancient method of preserving fruit (their origins are probably in the Middle East), are appreciated all over South America. Because they are quite astringent, quinces are seldom eaten raw.

Rice (arroz in both Spanish and Portuguese) arrived in Spain and Portugal when the Moors took over. By the mid-fifteenth century, it had traveled from Aragon to Naples and one hundred and fifty years later it was one of the first crops introduced to South America. Particularly in Brazil, it is now a staple food, eaten almost daily.

Rice flour contains no gluten and is used as a thickener in some South American recipes. Plain, unsweetened rice flour is available at health-food stores. The sweetened variety sold in Oriental markets is not the same. In Spanish it is called *harina de arroz*.

Star apples (crisofillo in Spanish; camito in Portuguese) are tropical fruits native to the New World. They range in color from white to purple and are about the size of our common apple. When sliced across, the seeds and the core make a star design in the center. They are seldom seen outside the tropics.

Sugarcane (caña dulce ó de azúcar in Spanish; cana de açúcar in Portuguese) arrived in Spain from India with the Moors and was taken by Columbus to Cuba. Today, Brazil is the world's leading producer.

Tamarind (tamarindo in Spanish and in Portuguese) is a pod-bearing legume related to peas and beans. The brown pods, usually sold partly open and frequently broken, are somewhat unattractive in the market. The yellow pulp between the seeds is the commodity. Combined with water and then strained, it produces a sour liquid that is enjoyed by South Americans in beverages, jams, and jellies.

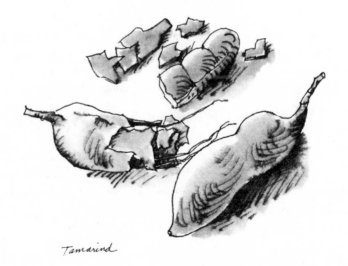

Tamarind

Tomatillos are not tomatoes but are related. They have an acidic, lemony taste, somewhat close to green tomatoes. *Tomatillos* are used raw or cooked, in salsas, ceviche, and stews.

Tomatoes (tomate in both Spanish and Portuguese) are indigenous to the Americas but were unknown to the Incas. When they first appeared in Europe they were thought by some to be the forbidden fruit from the Garden of Eden and were dubbed love apples. Because tomatoes are members of the nightshade family, Europeans also believed they were poisonous and for many years tomatoes were grown only as decorative plants.

Turkeys are native to Mexico. The Aztecs called them *uexolotl*, a name so unpronounceable that, we might say, another was needed. The Spanish call them *pavo*; the Portuguese, *peru*. Most of the stories about other names are interesting, whether or not they are entirely true. The Spanish took the bird to Spain and from there it went to England. From England it was returned to the New World, this time to North America. The Portuguese took the turkey to Goa, their colony on the coast of India, where the local natives believed it came from Peru (they remembered the potato) and they called it a *peru*, a name still in use wherever Portuguese is spoken today. In France, it is called *dinde* which is believed to be a corruption of *coq d'Inde*.

The name *turkey?* Well, the bird first arrived in England (some sources say) with merchants who had called not only in Seville where they picked up the turkeys but also at Turkish ports in the eastern Mediterranean. The English called these traders Turkey merchants and their feathered cargo Turkey birds.

Vanilla (vainilla in Spanish; baunilha in Portuguese) is native to Mexico and Central America. The flavoring essence or liquid is extracted from the cured pod of a climbing orchid and was in use by Montezuma at the time of the Conquest. He had, by then, also discovered the magic combination of vanilla and chocolate.

Chili Pepper Primer

The original Nahuatl (Aztec) Indian word is *chilli*; the Spanish word is *chile*; most modern English dictionaries prefer the word chili—that is my choice as well. When it comes to common names to distinguish the myriad varieties, there is so little consensus that the orderliness of botanical nomenclature becomes instantly appealing. However, they do not speak Botany in the markets, in the grocery stores, or in recipe books. The following primer is a guide; you may well find other names in other places.

The foods of South America, taken as a whole, are not fiery hot and on any scale they fall behind those of the real chili-pepper eating countries—India, Thailand, Mexico, and parts of China. Even so, the pungent, flavorful capsicums do play an important role in South American cooking.

Chili peppers are among the oldest cultivated plant foods indigenous to the New World. They originally grew wild and they still do, but historians believe chilies were domesticated long ago, and that it probably happened in Mexico and Peru at about the same time. Archaeologists tell us they were cultivated in Mexico nine thousand years ago and we have evidence that they were grown in Peru and Brazil by 6500 B.C. In Peru, traces of ancient chilies have been found at the prehistoric sites at Ancón and Huaco.

Chili peppers are botanically unrelated to *piper nigrum*, the spice but, in the time-honored tradition whereby new things are named after others they resemble (or seem to resemble), chilies were labeled "peppers" soon after their discovery.

We will never know what convinced primitive man to continue eating chili peppers after he took the first explosive bite, but we do know that humans are unique in their persistence in eating initially unpalatable foods. We also know that tolerance to chilies is acquired. Today they are consumed regularly—and in quantity—by one fourth of the world's adult population. They are, in fact, the most widely used seasoning in most of the Third World.

27

Chilies remained a Western Hemisphere secret until Columbus discovered them on his first voyage to the New World. In 1493 he introduced them to Spain where they became known as *pimientos de las Indias*. Once the Portuguese were established in what is now Brazil, they shipped quantities of the fiery fruit to their other colonies in the East Indies, Africa, and India. Acceptance of chilies as food in Europe was not immediate. At first they were grown almost exclusively in monastery gardens as ornamental plants. Later, the invading Turks reintroduced chilies to Europe, this time as a condiment.

By 1526 they were known in Italy, in Germany by 1543, and they were brought to North America by the British colonists. As early as 1618, a type of chili powder was available in England, but it was not until Victoria's reign and the British love affair with Indian curries and chutneys, that the chili peppers reached their full culinary status in England. Today, chili peppers are grown in tropical and subtropical regions throughout the world. In these hot countries, they not only flourish, but they are most appreciated.

Their numbers are legion. Many varieties are almost alike—but not quite. The most widely used condiment in the world, they have different names in different places. They hybridize, naturalize, and spread with ease. Not only do the names change constantly, so do the fruits themselves. It is not unusual for one name to be used, at least in popular parlance, for several varieties. Conversely, different names are frequently given to the same variety—one if it is fresh, another if is dried. Descriptions are helpful, but only to a point. One person's "mild" may be another person's "hot." Small, medium, and large are also subjective assessments.

All chilies belong to the genus *Capsicum*, mainly the species *annuum*, *chinense*, and *frutescens*. All are members of the large and diverse Solanaceae family, which also includes tomatoes, potatoes, eggplant, tobacco, and the deadly nightshade. There are many varieties of peppers within each species. It has been estimated that more than a hundred varieties and cultivars (man-made varieties) are grown in Mexico today and over two hundred worldwide. *Ají*, a Spanish version of the West Indian Arawak word *axi*, is the general name given to all Andean peppers today. In Peru, many of the Quechua and Aymara names are still used for individual varieties.

All chilies, whatever their variety, share a number of common characteristics. They range in color far beyond what we generally find available in our local markets and span the spectrum from pale to dark green to orange, yellow, red, ivory, and purple. Contrary to most perceptions, many green chilies taste hotter than red ones because when some chilies are ripe (red, in most cases), they develop a sweetness that balances the heat. When chilies are dried, the flavor becomes more robust and concentrated.

It is most often, but not always, true that the smaller the chili, the darker the color, and the more pointed the end the greater the heat. Chili peppers range from hot to hotter to hottest, although we seldom find any hotter than hot in our markets. Many growers and processors rank all chilies on a scale from one to one hundred twenty; popular *jalapeño* rates only fifteen.

Capsaicin is the active ingredient responsible for the heat. It is a pungent, reddish, oily substance closely related to vanillin. Capsaicin was first isolated in 1876 and first diagrammed chemically by Elnathan Kemper Nelson, an American chemist, in 1919. Capsaicin appears as tiny blisters on the interior ribs of the chili. When disturbed, that is, handled, it spills over onto the nearby seeds causing them to be hot as well.

Contradictory as it may seem, it is the heat that makes chili peppers an attractive food in hot climates. When eaten, the fiery fruits cause the heart to beat faster. This induces sweating that, in turn, cools the body and reduces its temperature. Studies show that South Americans suffer little heart disease, a fact that has been attributed to their consumption of chili peppers. Chilies have the additional advantage of being low in calories, of facilitating the digestion of starches, and of stimulating the appetite. They are rich in vitamins A and C, but are rarely consumed in quantities large enough to make an appreciable difference in the diet.

Handling Fresh Chilies

Chili peppers must be handled with care to prevent painful skin, eye, and nose burns. Some people wear rubber or plastic gloves whenever they handle fresh chilies. Certainly, it is a practical idea if large quantities are being prepared because continued contact with the capsaicin can cause the hands to become painfully red and actually burned.

If rubber gloves are not worn, wash hands well in warm, soapy water before and after handling chilies and, definitely, before handling anything else. Rubber gloves or no, scrub all boards and utensils well after use. Keep hands away from the face while handling chilies and exercise exceptional care if you wear contact lenses. Because it is the volatile oil in the fresh chilies that causes the burning reaction, there is less (but still some) danger when working with dried varieties.

The fact that most chili peppers are hand picked is partly responsible for the relatively small size of the crop that is grown in the United States. The most important reason, however, is that the demand is relatively low. In North America, interesting selections of fresh chilies are to be found in retail markets only where the population demands them for daily use. The dried varieties are more widely distributed. As the availability of more varieties, both fresh and dried, increases, proper home storage becomes important.

Storage

Dried chili peppers, in good condition keep indefinitely when stored in an air-tight container and kept in a cool, dry place. The easiest and most reliable method is to close them tightly in plastic bags and store them in the refrigerator. Because air and moisture are damaging, check a stored bag every six weeks or so to be sure the contents are free of bugs and moisture.

Bottled chili powders deteriorate rapidly when exposed to air and light, so should be kept in drawers or cabinets.

Fresh chilies are easily stored. Wrap them, not touching one another, rolled in paper towels and place in the refrigerator. Plastic bags are not recommended. Properly stored, fresh chilies keep well for up to two weeks. They also freeze successfully, but must first be blanched in boiling water for ten minutes. To reduce their pungency somewhat, soak fresh chilies in cold, salted water for an hour.

Roasting Chilies

Roasting and peeling bell peppers and chili peppers removes any bitterness (which is in the skins) and concentrates the flavor and sweetness. The flavor, as opposed to the heat, is in the flesh and varies according to variety, but strong color and flavor usually go hand in hand. Mature chilies can be as much as fifty percent more pungent than immature ones.

The roasting process takes a little time, but it is not difficult and the results are rewarding. Over a gas flame or under an electric broiler, char the fresh chilies thoroughly on all sides. Do this by holding them with a long-handled kitchen fork over the gas flame or by placing the chilies on a foil-lined cookie sheet set about three inches from the electric broiler. When the chilies are *completely* charred, collapsed, and quite awful looking, place them in a brown paper bag, close it tightly, and allow the chilies to steam in the bag (away from the heat) for about twenty minutes. Then, pull out the stems, brush away the seeds, and peel off the charred skin. Do not rinse away the skin and seeds under cold running water. It simply washes away the good juices, together with the seeds and skins. Roasted chilies keep, tightly covered in the refrigerator, for about a week. They also freeze beautifully.

Home canning of chili peppers is *not* recommended. Because they are low-acid fruits, an extremely high canning temperature is required to kill all bacteria. The risk is not worth it.

Preparing Dried Chilies

The traditional method of preparing dried chilies for use is to remove the stems, shake out the seeds, rinse them well, break the pods into pieces, and soak them in warm water to cover for about thirty minutes—longer if the pods are very dry. When they have soaked long enough, purée the chilies with enough of the soaking liquid to make a smooth paste. A blender or food processor works well.

The African cooks of Bahia almost always make a paste of soaked dried chilies mixed with fresh garlic, salt, and other spices and condiments.

Dried Pasilla pepper

They combine them with a mortar and pestle but the chore takes only a few seconds in a blender or processor.

In Latin America, chilies are sometimes smoke-dried by a process that dates to Aztec times. Dried in this way, they are called *chilpotle*, the Nahuatl word. Chilies in Latin America are sometimes sold with the seeds removed. They are then called *capónes* or castrated ones.

Although the guideline mentioned above—the smaller, more pointed, and darker in color the chili, the greater the pungency—may often be true, do not depend on it. Appearances are not always true indicators and it is quite possible for different fruit from the same plant to vary in hotness. Genetics controls the heat *range*, but not the exact amount, for each variety. Specific growing conditions dictate the precise heat within a given range. Any cookbook writer bold enough to list exact quantities of chilies required for particular recipes looks for trouble. Tastes vary considerably. Personal experimentation is the only satisfactory solution. Keep in mind while experimenting that the heat of cooking intensifies the chili's natural heat. Many varieties of chili pepper are interchangeable in cooking—a useful attribute. In the following descriptions, acceptable substitutions are noted.

Anaheim peppers are frequently available in our markets, but they have little to do with South America. Emilio Ortega, who set up a cannery in the city of Anaheim, first brought them to Southern California from New Mexico. The green *chiles verdes* are the immature fruit. Ripe and red, they are *chiles colorados*. Of somewhat ordinary flavor, these mild to hot chilies are grown extensively in California and the Southwest. They range from five to eight inches in length and, although sometimes marketed as *guajillo* chilies, they are not the same.

Anchos are dried *poblanos* and among the most commonly used dried chilies. In the Mexican state of Baja California and in parts of the western United States, both the fresh and dried *poblanos* are known as *anchos*. Sometimes, they are also called *pasillas* but that is a different chili. *Mulato* is another name for dried *anchos* and this is the name used by growers in the United States when referring to the dried chili pods. They call the fresh green chilies *anchos*. Whatever the name, they are a year-round crop in Southern California. The word *ancho* means "broad" in Spanish and this chile is well named. Triangular, four to five inches long and about three inches wide, it is dark reddish brown. Slightly hot, with a good flavor, it is almost always soaked, then ground to a paste for cooking.

Aji Amarillo means "yellow chili" in Spanish. Although this fiery hot variety is the most popular chili in Peru, it does not grow well north of the equator and is seldom seen in the United States. In Peru, where it is generally ground, it is considered a necessary ingredient for authentic *anticuchos*.

Banana Peppers are often confused with Hungarian yellow wax peppers although they are not the same. Banana peppers are sweet; Hungarians are hot. Both are usually available in our markets, especially in the fall. When fully ripe, they both turn red and the Hungarian becomes too hot to eat.

Bell Peppers are consistently popular in the United States but are used very little in South American cooking. Mild, and available year-round, they may be purchased green, yellow, red, or purple. The red ones have ripened on the vine and are sweeter than the green ones, which are immature and unripe. Golden yellow ones are mature, sweet, and mellow. Purple bells, relatively new to the market, are unripe and are green inside. If left on the vine, they will gradually turn green and then red. The purple skin becomes a dull green when cooked. In the Midwest, bell peppers are sometimes referred to as *mango peppers*.

Cayennes, although they probably originated in French Guiana and were probably named after that country's Cayenne River, are not cultivated in South America today. They are easy to grow, are available year-round and are raised extensively in the United States—especially in the South, where French Creole and Cajun cooking originated. The thin, 3- to 8-inch-long, tapered pods are very hot and they continue to ripen (or at least to become hotter) after being pickled. Beware of commercial powdered "Cayenne Pepper," which may not contain a trace of the real thing. *Cayennes* closely resemble the hot South American *mirasol* for which they are a good substitute. They can also be used instead of *habañeros*, *jalapeños*, and *serranos*.

Chilpotles are chilies for which there are no substitutes. They are ripened, dried, and smoked *jalapeños*, a dark reddish-brown, tapered, and twisted. Although quite tiny, usually about two inches long and less than one inch wide, they pack a large amount of heat into their small size. They are available in Latin markets either dried or bottled in vinegar. Bottled varieties should be rinsed and drained before using.

Fresnos are medium-sized, cone-shaped chili peppers that are widely available in the United States—probably because they were developed here and are grown here almost exclusively. About an inch and a half long and tapered, they are generally sold green, but will turn red when fully ripe. *Serranos* are a good substitute.

Guajillos are, properly, not dried *Anaheims* (although they are sometimes sold in the United States under that name), but the dried version of the *mirasol*. They are sometimes called *cascabel* as well. Those called *guajillo* are generally longer, four to six inches, and those called *cascabel* are generally rounder, about two inches in diameter, although the size of the fruit varies considerably. Both impart a yellowish color to foods with which they are cooked and both are exceptionally hot. *Guajil-*

los were known and grown in pre-Columbian times and are grown in Mexico and Peru today.

Güero in Latin-American countries sometimes becomes a generic name for yellow peppers because it means *blonde* in Spanish. True *güeros*, which are mature but not fully ripe at the yellow stage, are available fresh in the United States in the fall and canned throughout the year. They are about two inches long, tapered and moderately pungent. Hungarian wax chilies can be substituted.

Habañeros are flavorful chili peppers that are probably the hottest available in the United States. Smaller than *jalapeños*, they originated in South America, or possibly in Cuba. The name may be a derivative of La Habana, Cuba's capital city, which we call Havana. In Jamaica they are known as Scotch Bonnets. *Habañeros* are used extensively in Brazil and in parts of the Caribbean in all stages of ripeness—green, yellow, and red. Sometimes they are available in the United States, bottled, from Trinidad. *Cayennes* may be substituted.

Hontaka chilies are another good substitute for the unavailable *mirasols*. They are red, dried, wrinkled, and extremely hot. Latin and Oriental markets sell them.

Jalapeños are the most popular and widely used chili pepper in the United States today. Available year-round, they are called *jalapeños* whether red or green, fresh, smoked, or pickled. In Mexico the fresh ones are known as *cuaresmeños* and the pickled ones are called *jalapeños*. If they are mature (red) and smoked, Mexicans call them *chilpotle*. And so the confusion continues. *Jalapeños* range from hot to very hot and are interchangeable with *serranos*. Medium to dark green, they are small and oval with tapered ends, smooth shiny skin, and quite thick, juicy flesh. They are popular in the United States for making *jalapeño* jelly, a sweet-hot condiment, as well as for cooking and are probably the most versatile chili available. *Cayennes* may be substituted.

Malaguetas are small, aromatic, and exceptionally hot. They are considered indispensable to Bahian cooking, but we must substitute the *tabasco* chili (or even the sauce), at least for the time being because *malaguetas* are not imported into the United States. The most important and frequently prepared Bahian sauces all list *malagueta* peppers among the ingredients.

Mirasols, the fresh, ripe version of the *guajillo*, are not yet available in the United States. They were given the musical name (which means "looking at the sun") because of the fruit's erect position on the plant. They date from pre-Columbian times when they were grown in both Peru and Mexico. They are extremely hot and, although *ají* is a common word used for all Andean chili peppers, *mirasol* is generally what Peruvians mean when they say "*ají.*" Green or yellow when immature, they turn a rich, dark brownish-red when fully ripe. *Serranos* and *hontakas* are good substitutes.

Mulato is another name for the dried *ancho* (also called *poblano*). Although they are the same shape as the *anchos*, *mulatos* are darker, larger, and hotter; some say they are sweeter. To complicate matters further, they are sometimes called *pasillas*. *Mulato* is actually a name given to many similar dried chilies. The pepper itself is four to five inches long, tapered, and frequently sold in bulk. Powdered *mulatos*, *anchos* and/or *pasillas* are often used in Latin American cooking.

Pasillas are much longer than *anchos*—up to six to seven inches, thinner, and wrinkled. When dried they turn a very dark brown. They are most often used dried and are then called *chiles chilacas* or, in Baja California and on Mexico's west coast, *chiles negros*. Some say they are "mild to hot." Others describe them as "hotter than the *ancho*." All agree that their flavor is good. *Poblanos* are a good substitute.

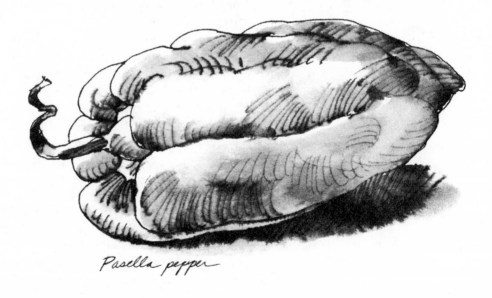

Pasella pepper

Pequíns are tiny, only about half an inch long, but are extremely hot. Used interchangeably with *guajillos*, the dried versions of the *mirasol*, they are sometimes known as *tepíns*. *Pequíns* are available, dried or canned, in Latin markets.

Pimientos have recently become available fresh as well as canned. The heart-shaped chilies are smaller, sweeter, and thicker fleshed than bell peppers and, with a distinctive aromatic flavor, they are a more interesting ingredient.

Poblanos take us back to *anchos*, of which they are the fresh, green version. In Mexico, where they originated and where they are the most widely used chili peppers today, the name *poblano* is applied to a large number of green peppers. Growers in the United States, in Southern California, call the fresh green chilies *anchos* (the dried they call *mulatos*). Although they are available canned in Latin markets, they are a year-round crop in California. *Poblanos* are about as large as bell peppers, somewhat more pungent, and have a much fuller flavor. They are shiny, heart-shaped, and a very dark green—almost black.

Serranos, bright green, one to two inches long, and tapered, are available fresh in the United States year-round and are also canned and pickled. *Serranos* are mildly hot to very hot, especially flavorful, and may be used interchangeably with *jalapeños* or as substitutes for *cayennes* and *Fresnos*.

Tabasco peppers are just over one inch long, tapered, bright red, and extremely hot. Whole peppers are bottled and marketed but it is Tabasco Sauce for which they are so widely known. Actually, the sauce was renamed after it had already become popular. Its inventor talked to someone recently returned from the Mexican state of Tabasco and found the name appealing. Edmund McIlhenny was not the inventor of the now-famous sauce, but he was the first to market it. That was just after the Civil War and it is still produced and bottled in Louisiana from the original recipe. In order to meet today's demands, it is now produced in Mexico, Central America, Venezuela, and Colombia as well.

National Dishes and Preferences

The huge southern continent of South America is one of enormous geographical diversity and includes ten major nations whose collective populations trace their ancestors around the world. Clearly differentiated eating habits exist between the wealthy few and the much poorer majority and national boundaries are not always important because cuisines south of the border are as often regional as they are national.

Empanadas are especially popular in Argentina and Brazil, but are also eaten in Bolivia, Uruguay, Chile, and the other countries as well. *Chupe de camarones*, the shrimp chowder so beloved by Peruvians, is almost as popular in neighboring Chile and Ecuador. Because it is an uncomplicated dish, allowing liberal discretionary powers to individual cooks, variations in each country are numerous. *Ceviche* is claimed by both Peru and Ecuador. If it really matters, they may both be correct, because fish "cooked" in citrus juice is an ancient tradition, known long before national boundaries divided the area. Brazil's ubiquitous manioc meal (*farinha de mandioca*) is indigenous and strictly Brazilian. Within the country it ignores all social barriers. It may not qualify as a national dish, but it is a national habit.

Earthy black beans, beloved especially, but not exclusively, by Brazilians and Venezuelans, are the basic ingredient in numerous classless dishes that also freely cross national boundaries. Although potatoes are ever-present on any list of Peruvian foods, most of the deliciously sauced potato dishes are regional rather than national specialties. *Papas chorreadas*, the rich and well-seasoned potato favorite from the Colombian highlands, is found, in remarkably similar forms, elsewhere.

Some countries do have recognizable national dishes and some of those dishes, Brazil's *Feijoada completa* for one, are ritual presentations of long standing. Others, although particularly popular and delicious or regionally distinctive, are not encumbered with the philosophical baggage of a National Dish. The descriptions of special South American dishes that follow are listed by country but few of the ingredients are restrained by national boundaries. In addition, the still-strong influence of the Iberian peninsula ensures that many of the dishes popular in one country are not unknown in others.

Colombia

With their feet, so to speak, in both the Caribbean and the Pacific, Colombians eat excellent seafood. *Pargo*, a fish similar to red snapper, is especially popular and so are the many versions of *Cazuela de mariscos*, a spicy mixed seafood casserole. *Sopa de pescado tunaco* (page 82) is a specialty of Tunaco, a small city on the Pacific coast, and *Soufflé de calabeza* (page 101) combines shrimp with summer squash in a luncheon or supper dish much like a soufflé.

Coast-dwelling Colombians depend on rice, but corn and potatoes are staples in the interior. Potato dishes, the sauce-drenched *Papas chorreadas* (page 150) among others, are often presented as separate courses as they are in Peru. *Ajiaco bogotano* (page 79), a rich, creamy chicken and potato soup-stew, qualifies as a national dish. *Empanadas*, often called *Pastelitos* (page 68) in Colombia, frequently include potatoes in the filling.

Colombians thrive on hearty combination dishes, *cazuelas* (casseroles), *cocidos* (stews), and *sancochos* (boiled dinners). Invariably, these include *choclo*, small pieces of corn on the cob that are a continental trademark and are popular in several other South American countries.

Corn also means *arepas*, a staple food of the poor in both Colombia and neighboring Venezuela, made from a special flour that is ground from very starchy, precooked corn. Because they are nothing more than a combination of cornmeal, salt, and water quickly cooked on a griddle, *arepas* are generally crisp on the outside and doughy on the inside. Sometimes they are cooked on a wire grill directly over the heat, a method that does nothing to improve their doughy interiors. They are not flat as *tortillas*, which are made from another type of precooked corn, but are thick, round and quite solid. Few of the tricks used to make *arepas* more palatable really do the trick for us. Even at their best—which is not the way they are eaten by most people—lightly seasoned, wrapped around a piece of fresh white cheese, and grilled until golden, they are merely pleasant. Yet, in much of South America these little corn cakes are not only a traditional food, they are, all too often, the only food in many poor homes.

Venezuela

Venezuela, with its tropical Caribbean coast, snow-capped mountains, dense rain forests, and oil-rich and internationally-oriented capital of Caracas, shares many cooking traditions with neighboring Colombia. *Arepas* are a staple food here, too, for the multitudes of poor whose put-together houses (charmingly called *ranchos*) cover the suburban hill-sides. Along the coast, coconuts and tropical fruits are abundant, as are excellent fish and shellfish. Pickled fish is popular. Plantains are served frequently.

Venezuelans know and use a number of root vegetables some of which are unfamiliar to us. *Apio*, which we know as celery root or celeriac is a special favorite. Whatever their social or economic standing, Venezuelans love black beans. *Caraotas negras*, (page 139) a simply prepared and especially popular version, is lovingly referred to as *caviar crillo* or native caviar. *Frijoles negros con jamon*, (page 140) another of the many variations, is also delicious. *Pabellón criollo*, (page 121) takes *Caraotas negras* a step further, combines it with shredded beef, rice, seasonings, bananas and, sometimes, fried eggs to produce a hearty meal that has been called Venezuela's national dish.

Brazil

Brazil, by far the continent's largest country, is the only one with a Portuguese heritage, and the only one in which slaves played a significant role. Even with three distinctive and distinct cuisines, those of Bahia, São Paulo, and the country as a whole, Brazilians all rally round their national dish, *Feijoada completa* (page 131). There is no one definitive recipe for this special feast but the many available differ from one another very little. Brazilians are also addicted to *empanadas* (which they call *empadas* or *empadinhas*) to manioc meal, and, as befits their Portuguese heritage, to confections and desserts rich and sweet with eggs and sugar.

The great dishes of Bahia have earned their reputations and are frequently enjoyed in the rest of the country as well. Internationally-oriented São Paulo, Brazil's "working" city, is known for its delightful version of *cuscuz* (couscous) (page 111), studded with vegetables and chicken or meat. Rice is far more popular than are potatoes everywhere in Brazil. Fish and shrimp, both fresh and dried are also important, especially in Bahian cooking. Nowhere in Brazil are vegetables or salads eaten in appreciable quantities. Exotic hearts of palm frequently garnish entrées and are made into delicious soups (page 75). Although grilled meat (*churrasco*), is cooked to order at popular restaurants called *churrascarias* throughout the country, Brazilians eat far less meat than do the citizens of Argentina and Uruguay.

Argentina and Uruguay

The food preferences of Argentina and Uruguay, the next two countries along the Atlantic coast, are similar. Both were, in fact, governed as a unit for many years but today are separated by the broad muddy waters of the Rio de la Plata. In these lands of the *gaucho* meat is a staple. In Argentina, with its vast pampas, meat means beef—and lots of it. In tiny Uruguay, beef is also important although a good deal of lamb is raised and eaten as well.

Steaks, properly grilled, are the most popular fare in both countries. Portions are consistently huge (*matambre* (page 122), the stuffed and filled flank steak popular in all of South America, is often served as an appetizer or as a first course), although the days when a steak arrived automatically at the table in an Argentine restaurant have largely passed. Special restaurants, called *parrilladas*, serve only grilled meat and are numerous in both countries. Mixed grills are also popular. Uruguay's *Biftik a la montevideo* (page 117), a sauced and simmered steak dish, is a pleasant change from the national obsession with grilled meat.

Stews and *carbonadas*, which are baked, also have their place and often contain a large variety of fruit and vegetables in addition to meat. The Argentines combine meat and fruit in a number of dishes with outstanding results. *Pastel de carne y durazno* (page 118) is a fine example.

Although neither country is without excellent seafood, it has not become an important part of their cuisines, prejudiced as they are toward meat. Instead, in deference to their Italian heritage (ninety percent of both populations trace their ancestry to Spain or Italy), pastas are almost always included on a restaurant menu. Dinners are late and desserts usually simple with pastries mostly reserved for the late-afternoon break.

Humitas (page 144), a seasoned corn purée popular all over South America, reaches special heights in Uruguay and Argentina. In Argentina, too, *empanadas* (page 59) come into their own.

Bolivia

If landlocked Bolivia has a national dish, it is the *salteña*, their spicy version of the *empanada*. The reason for a different name in Spanish-speaking Bolivia, so the story goes, is that, years ago, a local woman visited the Argentine city of Salta and became enamoured of the savory pastries made there. Returning home, she gave the name *salteña* to her version of the *empanada* and the name spread throughout the country. Most *salteñas* are filled with a mixture of chopped beef, potatoes, raisins, olives, hard-boiled eggs, and *ají*—a great deal of *ají*. Bolivians like their food *picante*.

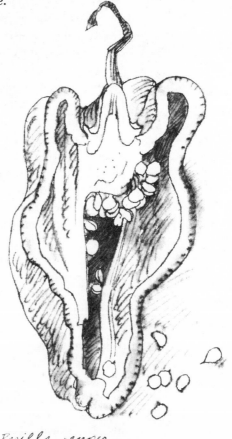

Pasilla pepper

This is meat and potatoes country for those who can afford meat. *Lomo montado*, a popular country dish, is simply a fried steak topped with a fried egg. High altitudes and cold nights make hearty soups and stews welcome at any season. *Pastel de choclo con relleno de pollo* (page 110), corn pie with chicken, and *Guisado de repollo* (page 142), spicy cabbage stew, are Bolivian dishes frequently served in cold weather.

Sopa de mani (page 76), an unusual peanut dumpling soup, is less hearty, but warming and nourishing just the same. *Anticuchos* (page 50), the marinated and grilled pieces of beef heart most often associated with Peru, are also popular here. Desserts in Bolivia are simple, most often tropical fruits that grow to perfection in the valleys.

Paraguay

South America's only other landlocked country, Paraguay, retains more of its Indian heritage and is infrequently visited by tourists. It is the home of *yerba maté*, the caffeine-laced herb tea popular throughout the southern part of the continent. The two national dishes are *Só o-yosopy* (page 82) and *Sopa paraguaya* (page 83). The Guarani Indian name, *Só o-yosopy*, is translated into Spanish as *Sopa de carne* and into English quite simply as beef soup. Often described as "comforting," it consists of little more than ground beef, a bit of rice, and seasonings. Although possibly not immediately appealing, on a cold, damp evening this thick, souplike dish is both nourishing and restorative. I believe that *Sopa paraguaya*, on the other hand, demands only better exposure to garner a following. Despite its name, it is not a soup but a delicious, cheese cornbread, often served with *Só o-yosopy*, but good with other dishes as well.

Chile

A continent away from the steamy jungles of the north, the tip of South America is a sparsely settled land of eternally snow-capped mountains, ice-blue glaciers, virgin forests, and wind-swept barrens. Most of the land belongs to Chile; some is part of Argentina. The southernmost extremes are closer to Antarctica than to any other major land mass.

Most of long, narrow Chile faces the Pacific Ocean and depends on the offshore Humboldt Current for some of the world's finest and most abundant seafood. In the central section of the country, a moderate climate, not unlike that in parts of northern California, nurtures vineyards, planted by missionaries in the sixteenth century, that produce the most drinkable wines made in South America. A wide variety of non-tropical fruits, including apples, table grapes, and lemons, are grown and are becoming increasingly important exports to North America where the seasons are reversed.

Chileans do not eat much meat. They have little grazing land. Even with the astounding variety of fish and shellfish available, a grand vegetarian stew of pre-Colonial origin reigns as their national dish. *Porotos granados* (page 167) based on Indian beans, corn, and squash supplemented with Spanish onions and garlic, is a fulfilling and surprisingly delicious one-pot meal.

Many Chilean fish and shellfish are both unknown and unavailable in our markets. Recipes, however, are adaptable. *Caldillo de congrio* (page 94), a fish stew, and *Chupe de camarones* (page 95), a shrimp chowder also popular in Peru and Ecuador, are delicious with our northern ingredients. *Sopa de berza* (page 80), a wonderful, cheese-rich, cabbage soup, and *Pastel de carne y pollo* (page 120), corn pie with meat and chicken, are other outstanding Chilean dishes.

Empanadas are frequently served as appetizers either with the acclaimed local wines or with the almost equally well-known *pisco*. Made only in Chile and Peru, *pisco* is a clear brandy distilled from grapes. Extremely alcoholic, it is usually best appreciated by most North Americans when combined with lime juice, sugar, and egg white in the drink called a *pisco* sour.

Peru

Neighboring Peru has, since its days as the heart of the Inca Empire, developed a sophisticated cuisine, one often ranked the best on the continent. Corn and potatoes, staples of the Inca diet, still are. Nowhere do potato dishes reach the culinary heights they do in the regional specialties of Peru. *Papa a la huancaina* (page 152), potatoes sauced with cheese, onions, and chili peppers, and *Papas arequipeña* (page 149), potatoes in a sauce of peanuts, cheese, and chili peppers, are fine examples and well worth trying. *Causa* (page 56), another specialty, resembles a well-seasoned and delicious mashed potato salad.

As they are in Bolivia, hot chili peppers, known generically as *ají*, are important to many dishes but when Peruvians say *ají*, they mean the fiery hot *mirasols*. Although the food is not generally as spicy as it is in Mexico, over all it is the hottest in South America. Specialties from the region around the city of Arequipa are the hottest of all. *Ají* and *ajo* (garlic) are the piquant Peruvian pair. Both lend their flavors to a popular dish called *Ají de gallina* (page 104), a chicken chili, and both are essential ingredients in the undisputed national snack or appetizer, *anticuchos*. Black beans show up again in the Peruvian repertoire. As *Frijoles negros escabechados* (page 141), they are pickled, delicious, and different.

Seafood is important to Peruvians and they do not lack variety. Small sections of corn-on-the-cob (*choclo*) invariably appear in soups and stews and are frequently used as an edible garnish. Peruvians love to embellish their food and most dishes are not considered ready for the table until they are imaginatively decorated with olives, hard-boiled eggs, sweet potatoes, tomatoes, onion rings, radishes, lettuce, and shrimp—and, of course, *choclo*.

Ecuador

North of Peru is Ecuador. True to its name, it straddles the Equator and has a mild climate in the highlands and tropical jungle along the coast. Bananas are a major crop. Seafood is plentiful. The *ceviche* of Ecuador is unique because it is made with the juice of bitter Seville oranges. *Chupe de camarón* is as much a part of Ecuador's cuisine as it is of Peru's. In both countries, guinea pig (page 135) is popular with the highland Indians. Hearty dishes such as a potato soup called *Locro de papas* (page 87) and a rich cheese and potato dish called *Llapingachos* (page 151)—pronounced yap-in-gachos—are delicious in our North American menus. Tropical fruits, the freshness and ripeness of which we may never know, and varieties of bananas we may never see here, are daily fare and frequently eaten as dessert.

Part II

Recipes and Menus

Appetizers
Entreméses; Aperitivos

Entremés literally translated, is "side dish," and this, it seems to me, is a more accurate way in which to describe most of the South American appetizers included here. They are, in fact, more akin to what I call first courses—small servings of rather substantial foods.

Most South Americans, especially those living in the cities, eat their midday and evening meals much later than we do, thus carrying on traditions of their colonial past. Ten or eleven o'clock is not considered late for dinner and, because South Americans frequently break their day in the late afternoon for coffee or tea and pastries, the cocktail hour with its savory finger foods is a less popular diversion there than it is here. However, the custom is coming into its own and canapés and dips borrowed from the international repertoire are considered sophisticated in many circles. Such foods have little in common with the authentic or traditional South American snacks, most of which are of pre-Columbian origin.

Anticuchos are street food. They are also interesting and delightful first courses or cocktail food. They probably date from before the Conquest when llama heart was used instead of the then unknown beef heart. *Ceviche* is familiar to many North Americans and it, too, is an ancient preparation that is just as successful today served as a first course at the table as it is served as a bite-sized morsel to go with drinks. The origins of the other appetizers in this relatively small section are less ancient. The codfish fritters are, without question, a legacy from the Iberian peninsula. *Empanadas*, which are a major attraction of South American cooking, demand special attention. I have given to them their own subsection among the appetizers.

Banana and Bean Dip

Entremés de Banana y Frijoles

2 *chorizo* or mild Italian sausages, skinned and chopped

1 onion, finely chopped

2 cloves garlic, pressed

2 or 3 *poblano* or other mildly hot chilies seeded, deveined, and finely chopped

½ cup tomato sauce (canned is acceptable)

2 cups cooked kidney beans, slightly mashed (if using canned beans include some of the liquid)

4 ripe, but firm, bananas, chopped

Tortilla chips for dipping

The first time I tried this appetizer dip, I knew it would be perfect for a Fall or Winter picnic or a tailgate party—and so it is. It is also an unusual side dish or, paired with a big green salad, more than adequate as a main course for a simple meal. This is not fancy food, but it is not ordinary either.

Sauté the sausage over medium-high heat for 5 minutes, stirring to prevent sticking and to break up the meat. Add the onion and continue to cook until the onion is soft. Reduce the heat to medium, add the garlic, chilies, and tomato sauce and cook for 5 minutes. Add the beans and bananas and enough of the bean liquid or water to make a thick, dip consistency. Mash the beans slightly with a potato masher and mix well. Cover and cook over low heat for 5 minutes.

Serve warm, with tortilla chips for dipping.

Yields 3 to 4 cups.

Beef Hearts, Marinated and Grilled
Anticuchos

1 beef heart

Marinade

6 to 8 cloves garlic, pressed

2 *serrano* or *jalapeño* chilies, seeded and minced

2 tablespoons ground cumin or cumin seeds, powdered

½ tablespoon dried oregano, crumbled

Salt and pepper to taste

1 ½ to 2 cups red wine vinegar

Sauce

⅓ cup dried *hontaka* chilies, seeded

1 teaspoon *annatto* powder, if available (see page 9)

1 tablespoon safflower oil

Salt to taste

Peruvians, whatever their status, love anticuchos *and frequently stop to buy them from street-corner vendors. No wonder. The aroma is seductive. The local residents, with their penchant for really hot, spicy food, dunk the pieces of marinated beef heart into a dipping sauce fiery with* mirasol *chilies. We must substitute* habañeros, jalapeños, *or dried* hontakas *but the results will probably be hot enough. Not familiar with beef hearts, I found when I first approached this recipe that a single one is large enough to make dozens of appetizers. Possibly, your butcher will sell you a portion of one if that seems more appropriate.*

Clean the beef heart thoroughly, removing all nerves and fat. Cut it into 1-inch cubes and place the cubes in a glass or stainless steel bowl.

To make the marinade, combine the garlic, fresh chilies, cumin, oregano, salt and pepper, and 1 ½ cups of the vinegar. Pour this over the meat. Add more vinegar, if necessary, to cover it completely. Marinate the meat in the refrigerator from 12 to 24 hours. Then, about 1 hour before grilling, remove from the marinade and thread on skewers. Reserve the marinade.

For the sauce, pull the stems from the dried chilies, shake out the seeds, and soak the pods in warm water for 30 minutes. In a blender or food processor, combine the chiles with the *annatto* powder, oil, and salt. Add enough of the reserved marinade (about ¾ cup) to make a thick sauce.

Brush the skewered meat with the sauce and grill it over hot coals or under a broiler, turning and basting to cook quickly on all sides. The *anticuchos* are best cooked medium-well, about 3 to 4 minutes on the grill. Serve with the remaining sauce for dipping.

Serves 10 to 16 as an appetizer.

Alternate method: Although the following method differs from the way it is done on the street corners of Lima, the result is both elegant and succulent. It may also be more appealing to those who doubt that *anticuchos* are delicious. Instead of cutting the heart into cubes, cut it into lengthwise strips about 2 inches wide. Cut the strips, again lengthwise, into long slices about ⅛-inch thick. Thread the long, thin slices on wood skewers in an undulating fashion. Marinating time should be cut to about 6 hours and they will cook to perfection very quickly, so watch them closely.

Peppers, Vinegar and cumin

Fish Kebobs, Marinated and Grilled
Anticuchos de Pescados

4 fillets or steaks of bass, cod, or other firm white fish

½ cup red wine vinegar

2 fresh *jalapeño* chilies, deveined and seeded

2 tablespoons olive oil

2 cloves garlic, peeled

½ teaspoon cumin seed

Salt and pepper to taste

Anticucho *may be translated as "food from the Andes cooked on sticks." These fish kebobs are not authentic* anticuchos *because fish was not a common food* from *the Andes. It was taken there, however, even in Inca times and it is available there today. These* anticuchos *make a nice first course or an entrée.*

Cut the fish into 2-inch cubes, removing any skin or bones. Place in a glass or stainless steel bowl and set aside.

Place the remaining ingredients in a blender or food processor and process until the chilies and garlic are puréed. Pour this sauce over the fish cubes and marinate in the refrigerator for 1 ½ to 2 hours.

Remove the fish cubes from the marinade, thread them on wooden skewers, and broil them over hot coals or under a broiler just until the fish flakes easily, probably no more than 3 to 4 minutes. Be careful not to overcook, and baste and turn the skewers frequently while they are cooking.

Serves 4.

Fish "Cooked" in Citrus Juice
Ceviche

Juice of 1 orange

Juice of 1 lemon

Juice of 4 limes

1 red onion, thinly sliced into rings

2 *ancho* chilies, or other mild, dried chilies, stems and seeds removed, crushed

½ teaspoon salt

2 medium fillets of red snapper, haddock, or other firm white fish

Lettuce, olives, parsley, cilantro for garnish

Ceviche *or seviche is popular throughout South America. More than one country claims to have originated this sophisticated dish but that perennial argument need not concern us.* Ceviche *is a wonderful, simple appetizer or first course and almost everyone likes it, including those who do not know (or believe) that the fish has been "cooked" in citrus juices instead of on the stove. In Ecuador* ceviche *is made with the juice of bitter Seville oranges, which unfortunately are seldom available here. A combination of orange, lime, and lemon juices produces a similar result and, even if not quite authentic, is very good. In Peru,* ceviche *is always served with lettuce and boiled sweet potatoes.*

Combine the orange, lemon, and lime juices. Blanch the onion rings in boiling water for 1 minute. Drain them, refresh immediately under cold water, and add them to the juices. Add the crushed dried chilies and the salt.

Cut the fish into bite-sized pieces, removing all skin and bones. Place it in a shallow glass or stainless steel, dish, cover with the marinade, and allow it to stand, at room temperature, for 4 to 6 hours. (If the weather is very warm, marinate the fish in the refrigerator.) The fish is "cooked" and ready to serve when the flesh becomes opaque.

To serve, arrange the fish pieces on lettuce leaves on a platter and garnish with olives and sprigs of parsley or cilantro.

Serves 4 as a first course.

Codfish Fritters with Green Onions and Cilantro
Bolinhos de Bacalhau

1 pound salt cod

2 tablespoons olive oil

½ cup green onions, minced

⅓ cup chopped cilantro

¼ teaspoon freshly grated nutmeg

½ teaspoon paprika

3 eggs, lightly beaten

2 cups mashed potatoes

Milk to mix

Salt to taste

Oil for frying

These mild salt cod and potato fritters are very popular in Brazil and I can attest to the fact that they are an almost perfect way to introduce salt cod to one who is wary. Serve as an appetizer with sliced or cherry tomatoes.

Soak the cod overnight in cold water, changing the water several times. Simmer it in fresh water for 10 minutes. Drain, cut into large pieces and remove any skin and bones.

Heat the oil and sauté the fish with the green onions until the fish flakes easily with a fork. Add the cilantro, nutmeg, paprika, eggs, and mashed potatoes. Add the milk gradually until the mixture is of a proper consistency to be formed into balls. Check the seasoning and add salt if necessary. Set the mixture aside to cool for 10 minutes.

Heat the oil in a deep fryer or in a deep pot. Roll the codfish mixture into balls about the size of a walnut and drop them into the hot oil. Fry until they are golden and crisp on the outside. Drain on paper towels and serve hot.

Yields approximately 2 dozen balls.

Grapefruit and Cucumber Salad
Salada Carioca

3 large grapefruit

2 medium cucumbers or 1
English cucumber

2 to 3 tablespoons sugar

Fresh mint

Paprika or finely ground dried
chilies

Lettuce leaves

This simple dish works equally well as a first course or as a salad. On a hot day, I can't think of anything more refreshing, wherever it turns up during the meal. Cariocans are what the residents of Rio de Janeiro call themselves.

Cut the grapefruit in half and remove the meat from the peel. Remove the membranes from around the sections.

Peel the cucumbers and cut them into quarters lengthwise. Remove the seeds by scraping them out with a spoon. (A grapefruit spoon works well.) Cut the cucumber quarters into slices.

Combine the grapefruit sections, cucumber slices, and the sugar in a bowl and refrigerate for at least 2 hours. Serve the salad in small lettuce-lined dishes garnished with mint and lightly dusted with paprika or ground chilies.

Serves 6.

Warm Mashed Potato Salad
Causa

1 onion, very finely chopped

Salt and pepper to taste

1 teaspoon finely ground dried chili pepper or chili powder

Juice of 4 lemons

12 medium boiling potatoes

1 tablespoon olive oil

2 or 3 *jalapeño* chilies, seeded and cut across into thin slices

3 hard-boiled eggs, quartered

12 black olives

1 pound *queso fresco* (or substitute *feta* cheese), cut into 1-inch cubes

The origins of causa *are Indian. Rather like a smooth, well-seasoned mashed potato salad, it is best served warm or at room temperature. As they do with so many dishes, modern Peruvians often almost smother this one with hearty garnishes.* Causa *can also be served as a side dish as it is in the Summer Picnic Menu, on page 197.*

Combine the onion, salt and pepper, dried chili, and lemon juice and allow the mixture to stand while the potatoes are prepared.

Peel the potatoes and boil them until they are soft. Drain them well and mash them until they are smooth. Add the onion and lemon juice mixture and beat it into the potatoes. Gradually add the olive oil. Gently fold in the *jalapeño* slices and place the mixture in a mold (a round bowl works well) or in a serving dish.

It may be unmolded immediately onto a platter, served from the dish, or simply place the mixture on a platter and shape it into a dome. Garnish with hard-boiled eggs, olives, and cubes of cheese. Other traditional garnishes are cooked shrimp, avocado slices, and small pieces of corn-on-the-cob.

Serves 6.

Avocado and Milk Cooler

Vitamina de Abacate

1 ripe avocado

3 cups cold milk

Sugar to taste

½ teaspoon vanilla extract

In hot, steamy weather it is easy to become addicted to vitaminas, *fruit and milk combinations prepared in a blender. They are popular throughout South America, especially in the tropics and especially in Brazil. Avocados whipped up to drink are particularly popular. Other fresh fruits that make good* vitaminas *are bananas, papayas, peaches, apricots, and best of all, mangos.*

Peel the avocado and remove the pit. Place all the ingredients in a blender or food processor (in this case a blender works best) and mix until the avocado is liquefied and the drink is frothy.

Serves 4.

Cheese Biscuits
Biscoitos de Queijo

One small potato, peeled and cooked

2 tablespoons butter

1 cup grated Swiss-type or Cheddar cheese

1 cup flour

½ teaspoon salt

½ teaspoon baking powder

Milk or beaten egg yolk

Unusual for a Brazilian recipe, these light and tasty biscuits contain potato. I like them best made with not-very-Brazilian Cheddar cheese.

Mash the potato and combine it with the butter and cheese. Sift the dry ingredients and add them to the potato mixture. On a lightly floured board knead the dough three or four times and then roll out to one-third inch thickness. Cut with a round cutter. Place the biscuits on an ungreased cookie sheet and brush the tops with milk or beaten egg yolk. Bake at 375 degrees for ten to fifteen minutes or until the tops are lightly browned.

Yields 10 to 12 biscuits depending on the size.

Empanadas

Empanadas, small savory turnovers or tarts, are among the great delights of South America. You may not always know exactly what is tucked inside the little pastry packages, but you are not likely to be disappointed. South Americans have had a long time to refine these savory treats because *empanadas* arrived on the continent with the Spanish and Portuguese settlers. They were probably introduced into the Iberian peninsula during the long Moorish occupation. Also, quite probably, they would have been invented if they were not introduced because they are closely related to the *pirozhki* of Russia, the *calzone* of Italy, and the filled pastry delights of just about every cuisine on earth. If a country does not have its own version, it begs, borrows, or steals one.

In South America these turnovers have many names: *empanadas* in the Spanish-speaking countries, except in Bolivia where they are called *salteñas*, and *empadas* or *empadinhas* in Portuguese-speaking Brazil. They are also called *empanitas*, *pastels*, and *pastelitos*. Much of the extended nomenclature boils down to little more than a collection of affectionate diminutives and they are used interchangeably. In Brazil, *empadinhas* fall under the generic heading of *salgadinhos*, which may be translated as "little salties," that is, what we might call appetizers, savories, or finger foods.

All over South America these popular snacks are sold in *confiterías* (sandwiches and pastries), *whiskerías* (liquor and sandwiches), and *sandwicherías* (sandwiches). *Picadas* specialize in appetizers. They are sold by street vendors and prepared in countless home kitchens. Most often they appear as turnovers but they can also be prepared as small tarts baked in tiny tins. In addition to other ingredients, they frequently contain chopped hard-boiled eggs and chopped or whole olives. Recipes for fillings are numerous enough for several books and it is easy enough to dream up your own. The only rules are that the fillings must be moist enough not to dry out while baking but dry enough that the finished product can be eaten as finger food. They are, by the way, a wonderful way to make leftovers glamorous. The recipe for *Picadinho de porco* (page 127), for example, would make an excellent filling.

Empanadas can be made bite-sized for appetizers and snacks or large enough to feed several people. The baked versions (*al horno*), which require little last minute work, can be prepared and cooked in advance and then frozen. To reheat, do not defrost. Simply bake in a 350 degree oven for approximately 30 minutes. Large sizes will take somewhat longer. They may also be deep fried (*fritas*).

Empanada pastry recipes are almost as numerous as filling recipes because every cook has a favorite. A very "short" pastry is necessary if the *empanadas* are to be made in tiny tart tins. If the pastry is to be rolled and cut, any good piecrust recipe is fine. An important point to keep in mind is that the dough for *empanadas* must be rolled as thin as possible, and they must be generously filled.

Empanadas of Chile

Cream Cheese Pastry

3 ounces cream cheese

½ cup butter

generous dash Tabasco sauce

Pinch salt

2 tablespoons toasted sesame seeds

¼ cup freshly grated Parmesan cheese

1 cup flour

Although Cream Cheese Pastry (as well as Flaky Pastry) can be used for any empanada *made as a turnover, this seasoned pastry is especially good with Maria's Pork Pastelitos and Hearts of Palm and Shrimp Empadas.*

Combine the cream cheese, butter, Tabasco sauce, salt, and sesame seeds in a food processor or mix by hand with a wooden spoon. Add the Parmesan cheese and the flour and combine well. Chill the dough for 30 minutes before rolling. Bake the filled *empanadas* at 450 degrees for 8 to 10 minutes or until they are nicely browned.

Yields 20 three-inch *empanadas.*

Flaky Pastry

2 cups flour

Dash salt

1 cup lard

Approximately ¼ cup ice water

Many South American cooks like to use lard to make a flaky pastry and this recipe is a good example. It may be used with any filling but is particularly successful for Chili and Beef Empanadas, *Ham* Empanadas, *and Salt Cod* Empadinhas.

Combine the flour, salt, and lard in a food processor or in a bowl using a pastry blender. When the lard and the flour are thoroughly mixed, add the ice water slowly until the dough reaches the desired consistency for rolling. It should be more rather than less sticky.

This dough may be sealed without being brushed with water. Simply press the edges of the turnovers together with the tines of a fork. Bake them at 375 degrees for about 25 minutes or until they are nicely browned. Serve warm.

Yields 2 dozen three-inch *empanadas*.

Short Pastry

½ cup heavy cream

4 tablespoons safflower oil

2 tablespoons baking powder

1 ½ cups flour

1 egg, lightly beaten

A good "short" pastry such as this one is necessary for empanadas *that are made in small tart tins. Any of the fillings can be used to fill pre-baked tart shells and they make an interesting change from the usual turnovers.*

Combine the cream, oil, and baking powder. Add the flour and mix with a fork until the mixture forms a mass. Knead it into a ball and allow the dough to rest in the refrigerator for 20 to 30 minutes.

Press two-thirds of the dough evenly into shallow muffin tins or individual tart tins that have been well oiled.

Roll the remaining third of the dough as thin as possible and cut it into rounds slightly larger than the tins. Place a round of dough over each filled tart and seal the edges by pressing them together.

Brush the tops with the beaten egg and bake at 350 degrees for about 30 minutes or until they are nicely browned.

Yields approximately 20 small tarts, depending on the size of the tins.

Chili and Beef Empanadas
Empanadas a la Criolla

⅓ pound ground beef

1 tablespoon olive oil

½ onion, finely chopped

2 cloves garlic, finely chopped

3 to 6 *serrano* or *jalapeño* chilies, seeded and finely chopped

1 tablespoon ground cumin seed

Salt and pepper to taste

2 tablespoons chopped parsley

2 tablespoons chopped cilantro

2 small tomatoes, peeled, seeded, and finely chopped

½ cup raisins

1 recipe Flaky Pastry (page 62)

10 pimiento-stuffed olives, cut in half

This creole-style filling, with its raisins, olives, and chilies, is similar to a picadillo.

Sauté the meat in the oil until it is no longer pink. Break up the large pieces. Add the onion, garlic, chili peppers, cumin, salt, and pepper and continue to cook over medium heat until the onion is soft. Add the parsley, cilantro, tomatoes, and raisins and cook until the mixture is quite dry. Cool.

Roll out the pastry dough and cut into approximately 20 circles each about 3 inches in diameter. Place half an olive on each round of dough. Add a spoonful of the filling and fold pastry over to form a half moon. Seal with the tines of a fork. Bake at 375 degrees for 25 minutes or until nicely browned.

Yields about 20 three-inch *empanadas.*

Ham Empanadas
Empanadas Rellenos de Jamón

1 large onion, minced

2 tablespoons olive oil

2 cloves garlic, minced

2 or 3 *poblano* or Anaheim chilies, seeded and minced

⅔ cup diced, cooked ham

2 hard-boiled eggs, chopped

2 tablespoons freshly grated Parmesan cheese

1 recipe Flaky Pastry (page 62) or Short Pastry (page 63)

10 pimiento-stuffed olives, cut in half

Use the Flaky Pastry to make empanadas *in the form of turnovers or the Short Pastry to make small tarts.*

Sauté the onion in the olive oil until it is soft. Add the garlic and the chili peppers and continue to sauté for 2 minutes. Remove from the heat and combine with the ham, eggs, and cheese.

To make turnovers using Flaky Pastry, roll out the dough and cut it into approximately 20 circles, each 3 inches in diameter. Place a small quantity of the filling and half an olive onto one half of each round of dough and fold the pastry over to form a half moon. Seal with the tines of a fork and bake at 375 degrees for 25 minutes or until nicely browned.

To make tarts with Short Pastry, roll out two-thirds of the dough, cut 20 circles each 3 inches in diameter (or whatever size you need to fit your well-oiled, shallow muffin tins or individual tart pans), and line the tins. Fill with the ham mixture and top each tart with half an olive. Roll out the rest of the dough as thinly as possible and cut another 20 rounds, this time slightly larger than the diameter of the tins. Place a round over each filled tart and seal the edges by pressing the pastry together. Brush the tops with beaten egg and bake at 350 degrees for about 30 minutes or until the tarts are well browned.

Yields about 20 three-inch *empanada* turnovers or about the same number of three-inch tarts.

Hearts of Palm and Shrimp Empadas
Empadas de Camarão com Palmito

3 tablespoons green onions, including green part, minced

1 tablespoon butter

1 tablespoon flour

1 cup milk

1 cup hearts of palm, chopped

1 cup cooked shrimp, chopped

2 tablespoons minced parsley

½ teaspoon paprika

2 hard-boiled eggs, finely chopped

1 recipe Cream Cheese Pastry (page 61)

The spicy Cream Cheese Pastry works well with this somewhat mild empanada filling.

Sauté the green onions in the butter until they are soft. Add the flour and cook, stirring, for 2 minutes. Add the milk and stir until the mixture thickens slightly. Remove from the heat and stir in the hearts of palm, shrimp, parsley, paprika, and eggs.

Roll out the chilled Cream Cheese Pastry dough and cut out approximately 20 circles each 3 inches in diameter. Place a spoonful of the filling on each round of dough. Fold it over to form a half moon and seal with the tines of a fork. Bake at 450 degrees for 8 to 10 minutes or until nicely browned.

Yields about 20 three-inch *empanadas*.

Salt Cod Empadinhas
Empadinhas de Bacalhau

6 green onions, minced

2 tablespoons olive oil

3 cloves garlic, minced

3 *serrano* or *jalapeño* chilies, seeded and minced

¼ cup minced cilantro

1 cup cooked, flaked salt cod (see page 18 for initial preparation)

1 recipe Flaky Pastry (page 62)

The Flaky Pastry complements this filling nicely.

Sauté the onions in olive oil until they are soft but not brown. Add the garlic and the chilies and continue to cook until the chilies are softened. Remove from the heat and stir in the cilantro and the salt cod. Check for seasoning.

Roll out the Flaky Pastry dough and cut out approximately 20 circles each 3 inches in diameter. Place a spoonful of the filling on each round of dough. Fold it over to form a half moon and seal the pastry with the tines of a fork. Bake at 375 degrees for about 25 minutes or until nicely browned.

Yields about 20 three-inch *empanadas*.

Maria's Pork Pastelitos
Pastelitos de Cerdo a la Maria

¼ pound pork butt or shoulder, ground or very finely chopped

2 carrots, peeled and finely chopped

2 potatoes, peeled and finely chopped

Safflower oil, if necessary

3 tomatoes, peeled, seeded, and chopped

1 onion, finely chopped

2 tablespoons minced parsley

4 tablespoons minced cilantro

1 tablespoon safflower oil

2 hard-boiled eggs, chopped

1 tablespoon capers, rinsed, drained, and chopped

Salt and pepper to taste

1 recipe Cream Cheese Pastry (page 61)

This recipe was given to me by Maria de la Calle Thorson who brought it with her from her native Colombia.

Sauté the meat, carrots, and potatoes in a small amount of oil if necessary, until the vegetables are tender and the meat no longer pink.

In another pan, sauté the tomatoes, onion, parsley, and cilantro in 1 tablespoon oil until the onions are soft. Combine the two mixtures and stir in the chopped hard-boiled eggs and the capers. Add salt and pepper.

Roll out the chilled Cream Cheese Pastry and cut out about 40 rounds each 2 inches in diameter. Place 2 tablespoons of filling on each of 20 rounds and cover the filling with the remaining rounds. Seal the edges of the pastry with the tines of a fork. Bake at 450 degrees for 8 to 10 minutes or until nicely browned.

Yields about 20 two-inch *empanadas*.

First-course Soups

Sopas

The soup recipes in this section have been separated from the more
hearty ones that follow because these light, first-course soups will stimu-
late your appetite rather than fill you up. South Americans are fond of
soups which they enjoy almost daily and their repertoire is a full one.

Several of the recipes in this section use ingredients that seldom find
their way into our North American soup pots—avocados, bananas, coconut milk, and peanuts. They provide flavor combinations that are interesting and distinctive. Any one of these soups will start a meal in an
unusual style.

Gourd soup bowl with coconut, bananas and peanuts

Fresh Apple Soup
Sopa de Manzanas

Argentina

4 large tart apples (pippin or Granny Smith), peeled, pared, and quartered

4 slivers lemon peel

Sugar to taste, about 2 tablespoons

Cold water to cover

2 egg yolks, beaten

¼ cup golden raisins, soaked in warm water, drained, and chopped (optional)

2 egg whites, beaten (optional)

Both Argentina and Chile raise and export apples. I ate this pale fruit soup, with its wonderful taste of fresh apples, in Buenos Aires one May— just as winter blew in. Since then, I have found it as useful as it is delicious. I have downed it hastily for breakfast and served it as a first course for brunch. I like it for dinner before a pork roast and I have even found it handy as a dessert, for which I add half a cup or so of softened, chopped dried fruit and a sprinkling of chopped nuts. Or, serve it with a wedge of sharp Cheddar cheese and a bowl of nuts. For a thicker soup, beat two egg whites until they form soft peaks and gently fold them into the warm soup just before serving.

Place the apples, lemon peel, and sugar in a saucepan with cold water to cover. Bring to a boil, reduce the heat, and simmer gently until the apples are very tender.

Press the mixture through a food mill or purée in a food processor. With a wire whisk, beat in the egg yolks. Add the raisins and the optional egg whites and serve warm, but not hot.

Serves 4 to 6.

Avocado Soup

Sopa de Aguacate; Sopa de Abacate

3 large ripe avocados

1 tablespoon fresh lemon juice

4 cups chicken stock, chilled
and all fat removed

Salt to taste

Tabasco sauce to taste

2 cups half-and-half

2 tablespoons minced cilantro

Avocados are plentiful and avocado soups are popular in South America. To preserve the delicate fresh avocado flavor of this version, make it no more than an hour before it is to be served and serve it chilled rather than icy cold.

Peel and seed the avocados. Reserve half of one for garnish. With a fork, mash the remaining avocado, adding the lemon juice. Combine this mixture with the chicken stock. Add the salt and Tabasco sauce to taste but keep in mind that flavors are less pronounced when cold. A wire whisk works well but the mixture may be combined in a blender or food processor if a smoother texture is desired. Stir in the half-and-half and check seasoning.

Refrigerate the soup until 15 or 20 minutes before serving time. Stir well and serve garnished with the remaining half of avocado, freshly sliced, and a sprinkling of minced cilantro.

Serves 4 to 6.

Chickpea Soup with Cumin and Cilantro

Sopa de Garbanzos

3 cups cooked chickpeas

2 onions, coarsely chopped

1 tablespoon cumin seeds, crushed

8 cups beef or chicken stock

2 tablespoons flour

4 tablespoons butter

1 cup half-and-half

Salt and pepper to taste

3 tablespoons chopped cilantro, or more to taste

Chickpeas, cumin, and cilantro are partners all over South America—as well as in India and the Middle East. I am extremely fond of this rich, satin-smooth soup that underscores the affinity of the ingredients for one another and is elegant enough to begin a fine dinner. If canned chickpeas are used (and they are quite acceptable), include the liquid and reduce the stock by two-thirds of a cup.

Heat the chickpeas, onion, cumin, and stock until the stock boils. Reduce the heat and simmer for 20 minutes. Purée the mixture in a food mill or blender and return it to the pot.

Mix the flour and 2 tablespoons of butter to a paste and add it to the soup in small pinches. After each addition whisk until smooth. Simmer the soup for 10 minutes.

Add the remaining butter and enough half-and-half to reach the desired consistency. Correct the seasoning and garnish each serving generously with cilantro.

Serves 6.

Fresh Corn Soup
Sopa de Choclo

2 onions, finely chopped

4 tablespoons butter

4 ears fresh corn, kernels cut off and cobs scraped (about 3 cups)

4 cups chicken stock

4 eggs, beaten

Salt and pepper to taste

2 cups half-and-half

3 tablespoons chopped cilantro

This soup is best when made from freshly picked corn. If that is not available, frozen corn kernels are a good substitute. Canned ones are not. This is unusual for a Peruvian soup because it contains no potatoes.

Sauté the onion in 2 tablespoons of the butter until soft. Add the corn and chicken stock and bring the mixture to a boil. Lower the heat and simmer it for 2 to 3 minutes.

Add the beaten eggs and the 2 remaining tablespoons of butter and continue cooking for another 2 minutes. It is important not to overcook because that would spoil the wonderful fresh corn flavor. Correct the seasoning, add the half-and-half, and heat through. Serve immediately, garnished with cilantro.

Serves 6.

Creamy Coconut Milk Soup

Sopa de Leite de Côco

4 tablespoons cornstarch

3 cups (or two 14-ounce cans) thick coconut milk (see page 16)

3 cups chicken stock

1 small onion, chopped

Salt to taste

1 cup half-and-half

Grated nutmeg to taste

1 avocado, thinly sliced

This is an exotic soup, but at the same time subtle. It is equally good hot, chilled, or served at room temperature.

Blend the cornstarch with the coconut milk. Heat the stock, onion, and salt. Just before the stock boils, add the cornstarch and coconut milk mixture, stirring well to blend. Cook over low heat until the mixture thickens slightly.

Add the half-and-half and continue cooking for a minute or two but do not allow it to boil. Strain the soup to remove the onion.

Serve with a grating of fresh nutmeg and a garnish of avocado slices.

Serves 6.

Hearts of Palm and Coconut Milk Soup

Sopa de Palmito e de Leite de Côco

4 tablespoons unsweetened rice flour (available at health food stores)

1 cup milk

6 cups chicken stock

Pinch freshly grated nutmeg

Pinch ground allspice

1 can (14 ounces) hearts of palm (*palmitos*)

3 egg yolks, beaten

1 cup thick coconut milk (see page 16)

½ cup coarsely chopped salted peanuts

Two Brazilian "staples," hearts of palm and coconut milk, are combined in this soup. Although neither one is overly assertive, for me, they suggest the mingled flavors of the tropics. If this soup is served chilled, give it fifteen or twenty minutes out of the refrigerator before serving so that the flavors can regain their importance.

Combine the rice flour with ¼ cup of the milk and mix to a smooth paste. Gradually add the remaining milk. Heat the stock, add the flour and milk mixture, the nutmeg, and the allspice, and cook over low heat until it thickens slightly.

In a food processor or blender, purée the hearts of palm with some of the thickened soup and whisk in the beaten egg yolks. Add the coconut milk. For a velvety texture, strain the soup through a fine sieve. To serve, reheat carefully, slowly whisking all the while to prevent curdling. Garnish with the chopped peanuts.

Serves 6.

Peanut Dumpling Soup
Sopa de Maní

1 cup peanuts, roasted and coarsely ground

4 tablespoons unsweetened rice flour (available at health food stores)

1 egg

2 tablespoons half-and-half

6 cups rich chicken stock, skimmed of all fat

2 tablespoons chopped cilantro

This light and unusual peanut soup has become one of my favorites. The tiny peanut dumplings hold their shape beautifully and their crunchy texture complements the simple goodness of a rich chicken broth. The quality of the chicken stock is very important in this recipe so do not be tempted to skimp.

Combine the ground peanuts and the rice flour in a bowl. In another bowl beat the egg with the half-and-half. Combine the two mixtures and mix well.

Heat the chicken stock just to the boiling point. While it is heating, form the peanut mixture into *small* balls—about half the size of a walnut. Drop the peanut dumplings into the hot stock, reduce the heat, cover, and simmer over low heat for 15 minutes.

Garnish with chopped cilantro just before serving.

Serves 6.

Sweet Potato and Banana Soup
Sopa de Batata Doce e Banana

2 ham hocks or meaty ham
bones

7 cups water

3 whole cloves

1 onion

½ teaspoon ground allspice

4 juniper berries (optional)

3 sweet potatoes, peeled and
quartered

½ teaspoon dried thyme

2 large, firm bananas, cut in
four pieces

4 green onions, including tender
green part, minced

Salt and pepper to taste

Additional finely minced green
onion tops or parsley for garnish

From the northern coast of Brazil, this soup is heavy with African over-tones. I have substituted bananas for plantains, which have a lot less fla-vor, because I prefer the taste and because I like the contrasts between the sweet potatoes and bananas and the salty ham and pungent onion.

Cover the ham hocks with water in a soup kettle. Stick the cloves in the onion and add it to the pot. Add the allspice and the juniper berries. Bring the liquid to the boil and skim, if necessary. Reduce the heat and simmer for 1 hour.

Remove the ham hocks, strain the broth, and return it to the pot. Re-move as much meat as possible from the bones and reserve it.

Add the sweet potatoes and the thyme to the pot and simmer for 20 min-utes. Add the bananas and simmer for another 5 minutes. When the sweet potatoes are soft, remove them from the broth and purée them in a blender or food processor with a little of the broth. Return the purée to the pot, add the ham taken from the bones and the green onions. Com-bine thoroughly and add salt and pepper to taste. Serve hot, garnished with green onions or parsley.

Serves 6.

Hearty Soups and Stews

Sopas y Cocidos; Sopas y Guisados

Most hearty soups and stews reveal their peasant origins in the list of humble ingredients. They are one-dish meals to feed hungry people. For me, those of South America are among the most satisfying dishes from the various southern cuisines. Cabbage, potatoes, corn, fish, and shellfish are basic ingredients and, whether they are called *sopas, guisados, cocidos* or *locros, caldos, caldillos,* or *chupes,* the results are both warming and delicious.

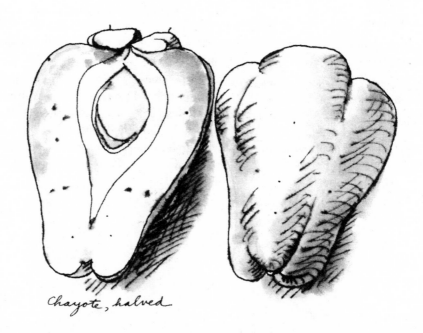

Chayote, halved

Creamed Potato and Chicken Soup

Ajiaco Bogotano

1 chicken (3 ½ to 4 pounds), cut up, or an equal weight of chicken pieces

8 cups chicken stock

1 onion, cut in half

1 bay leaf

½ teaspoon cumin seeds, ground

¼ teaspoon thyme

Salt and pepper to taste

2 pounds assorted potatoes, peeled and coarsely chopped

3 ears of corn, cut into 2-inch slices

1 cup heavy cream, at room temperature

2 tablespoons capers, drained and rinsed

1 avocado, thinly sliced

In Colombia, Ajiaco Bogotano is almost a national dish and local cooks, who have a wide choice, generally include more than one kind of potato when they make it. Our options are fewer, but improving all the time, and it is such a good dish that I wish everyone would try it. If possible, use a combination of the following potatoes: russet, red, white, yellow Finnish, and fingerling. Proportions are not important, but the total should be about two pounds. Even if you use only one kind of potato, the result will be a delicious, thick stewlike soup—a hearty meal in a soup plate and perfect for the proverbial dark and stormy night.

Combine the chicken and the stock and bring it to the boil. Add the onion, bay leaf, cumin, thyme, and salt and pepper. Reduce the heat and simmer, uncovered, for 30 minutes or until the chicken is very tender.

Remove the chicken from the stock and take the meat from the bones. Cut the meat into thin strips and discard the skin and bones.

Strain the stock and return it to the pot. Bring it to the boil, add the potatoes, and cook them until they are very soft and can be mashed against the side of the pot. Add the corn and the chicken meat and simmer, uncovered, just until the corn is cooked, about 5 minutes.

To serve, divide the cream and the capers among 6 generous soup plates. Add the soup, garnish with thin slices of avocado, and serve immediately. Or place the chicken meat, corn, sliced avocado, cream, and capers into separate serving bowls. Ladle the soup into 6 generous soup plates and let the diners add what they like to the basic soup.

Serves 6.

Cabbage Soup with Cheese and Spices
Sopa de Berza

2 tablespoons butter

1 small green cabbage, finely shredded, core discarded

1 large baking potato, peeled and finely chopped

3 green onions, finely chopped, including some of the green

5 cups chicken stock

Pinch freshly grated nutmeg

Pinch allspice

Salt and pepper to taste

1 cup grated Münster cheese

Paprika

Cabbage and potatoes are homey fare but here they are the perfect foil for the rich, stringy cheese. This soup is one of my favorites and I like to make it just before I serve it. The cabbage remains slightly crisp and when the cheese is added at the very last minute it arrives at the table half melted, gooey, and delicious.

Melt the butter in a large pot. Add the cabbage, potato, and green onions and toss to coat the vegetables well. Cook and stir for 3 to 4 minutes.

Add the stock and simmer, covered, for about 30 minutes or until the cabbage is crisp-tender. Do not overcook and allow the cabbage to become soggy. Season to taste with the nutmeg, allspice, and salt and pepper and stir in the cheese just before serving. Dust each serving with paprika.

Serves 6.

Corn Soup with Prawns
Sopa de Milho com Camarão

Brazil

2 pounds raw prawns or shrimp, shelled and deveined

2 cloves garlic, pressed or finely minced

5 cups chicken stock or fish stock or a combination

8 ears corn, scraped (about 2 cups kernels)

2 onions, finely chopped

2 tablespoons butter

1 teaspoon paprika

2 egg yolks

1 tablespoon lemon juice

Sliced avocado for garnish

This fresh tasting soup is a favorite in São Paulo, Brazil's phenomenal megalopolis.

Chop the shrimp coarsely, combine them with the garlic, and allow the mixture to stand for 10 minutes.

Heat the stock, add the corn, and simmer gently for 2 to 3 minutes.

Sauté the onions in the butter. Sprinkle with paprika. When soft, add the prawns and toss to heat. Add the onions and the prawns to the stock and reheat but do not allow it to boil.

Beat the egg yolks with the lemon juice and quickly whisk them into the soup. Serve at once with a garnish of sliced avocado.

Serves 6.

Paraguayan Beef Soup
Só o-Yosopy

1 pound lean sirloin, very finely ground

2 cups cold water

1 onion, finely chopped

1 small *poblano* chili, seeded and finely chopped

1 tablespoon olive oil

¼ cup raw rice

½ teaspoon oregano

1 tablespoon chopped parsley

Salt to taste

This is one of those dishes that are sometimes referred to as "comforting." No doubt it is good for you and it may even be enjoyable for those who relish boiled beef. It is not to my taste.

The name, translated from the Guarani Indian, simply means "beef soup." If you have a food processor or meat grinder, grind the meat yourself. If not, have the butcher run it through his machine twice because it must be very finely ground. It is also important to add the salt last to keep the meat and the liquid from separating.

Combine the meat and the cold water and mix thoroughly. Sauté the onion and the chili in the oil until the onion is soft. Add the meat, rice, and oregano. Cook over medium heat, stirring constantly, until the rice is cooked. This will take about 15 minutes. Do not allow it actually to boil. Add more water, if necessary. Add the parsley and the salt and serve with *Sopa paraguaya* (page 83), the traditional accompaniment.

Serves 4.

Paraguayan Corn Bread
Sopa Paraguaya

½ cup finely chopped onion

2 tablespoons butter

¾ cup corn kernels

¾ cup yellow cornmeal

¾ cup small-curd cottage cheese

¾ cup grated Münster cheese

½ cup buttermilk

½ teaspoon salt

3 eggs, separated

Sopa paraguaya is not a soup, and the reason for so misleading a name is lost in Paraguayan culinary history. This sopa is a cornbread and is popular throughout Paraguay. Recipes for it vary, but most call for both puréed raw corn and cornmeal, which make the finished product more solid than our basic cornmeal bread.

I like this version because the cottage cheese and buttermilk help to keep it light. Freshly scraped corn kernels are best but frozen (and thawed) kernels work well enough. Traditionally, Sopa paraguaya is served Só o-Yosopy (page 82). It also freezes well.

Sauté the onion in butter until it is soft. Purée the corn kernels in a blender or food processor and combine them with the cornmeal, sautéed onion, cottage cheese, Münster cheese, buttermilk, and salt. Mix thoroughly.

Beat the egg yolks until they are thick. Beat the egg whites until they form soft peaks. Fold the yolks carefully into the whites. Add one-third of the egg mixture to the corn mixture and combine well. Then carefully fold in the remaining egg mixture.

Pour the batter into a buttered 8- by 8- by 2-inch pan and bake at 400 degrees for 30 minutes or until it is nicely browned and tests done. Serve warm with butter.

Serves 4 to 6.

Fish Soup from Tunaco

Sopa de Pescado Tunaco

Colombia

2 pounds bass, cod, snapper or other firm white fish

Juice of 1 lemon

Salt to taste

2 onions, coarsely chopped

2 tablespoons olive oil

3 to 4 *jalapeño* or *serrano* chilies, seeded and chopped

6 tomatoes, peeled, seeded, and chopped

4 cups water or stock

2 cups coconut milk (see page 16)

Chopped cilantro

Tunaco is a city on Colombia's Pacific coast just north of the border with Ecuador, and this wonderful soup is one of its specialties. Because it cooks quickly, it retains its fresh taste. It also follows the rule of so many South American dishes by beginning with a thick onion and tomato sauce. Fish or chicken stock used in place of the water will yield a richer soup.

Cut the fish into bite-sized pieces. Sprinkle them with lemon juice and salt and set aside.

In a soup pot, sauté the onions in olive oil until they are soft. Add the chilies and tomatoes and cook over low heat for 2 to 3 minutes. Add the water or stock and the fish and simmer gently until the fish is almost done. Take care not to overcook. Add the coconut milk and let the soup come just to the boil. Serve immediately, topped with chopped cilantro.

Serves 6.

Locros

Thick, well-seasoned *locros* are a specialty of the South American continent. They are substantial dishes that can contain a single one or a combination of meats, fish, or shellfish. They always include a grain, potatoes, or other starch—or a combination of them. Some *locros*, those made with wheat or cornmeal, are probably indirectly descended from the North African *couscous*, which is also popular (in its more recognizable form) in Brazil.

The number of other ingredients included in a *locro* varies with the cook, the country and the occasion. There are not many rules but almost always the result is a delicious, hearty soup-stew, a one-pot meal of generous proportions with a particularly South American flair.

Green Corn Soup

Locro de Choclo

6 ears of green or very tender young corn

1 onion, finely chopped

½ cup olive oil

2 cloves garlic, minced

2 tomatoes, peeled, seeded, and coarsely chopped

1 green pepper, sweet or hot, roasted, peeled, seeded, and cut into strips (or use canned pimiento)

Salt and pepper to taste

6 small yellow crookneck squash, coarsely chopped

Parsley or cilantro for garnish

Locros *always include a grain or a starch. This Argentine version is especially satisfying if freshly picked green corn is available. Ordinary corn-on-the-cob is acceptable, but try to select tender young ears.*

Shuck the corn. Split the kernels with a sharp knife and scrape them into a dish, saving as much of the liquid as possible.

Sauté the onion in the oil until it is soft. Add the garlic, tomatoes, and pepper strips, and salt and pepper cook slowly for 5 minutes. Add the corn and enough water to reach the desired consistency. The stew should be quite thick. Bring the mixture to the boil, add the squash, reduce the heat, and simmer gently for 20 minutes. Serve in soup plates and garnish with parsley or cilantro.

Serves 6.

Potato Soup with Fish and Cheese
Locro de Papas

4 tablespoons butter

1 teaspoon paprika

2 onions, finely chopped

4 cups water

10 small baking potatoes, peeled and diced

2 cups half-and-half

½ pound firm white fish (haddock, bass, or cod), cut in bite-sized pieces

2 eggs, lightly beaten

1 ½ cups grated Münster cheese

Salt and pepper to taste

This locro, *with its potato base, is popular in the highlands, not only in Ecuador, but in the other Andean countries as well. Shellfish or meat can be substituted for the fish—or they may all be left out. A generous plate of sliced avocados is a typical accompaniment.*

Melt the butter in a large saucepan and add the paprika. Sauté the onions in this mixture until they are soft. Add the water, bring it to a boil, and add the potatoes. Simmer gently until the potatoes are almost done. Depending on the size of the potatoes, it may be necessary to add more water during cooking. Add the half-and-half and the fish and continue cooking, stirring occasionally, until the potatoes begin to fall apart. If they remain very firm, mash them gently in the pan with a potato masher or a wooden spoon.

Add a little of the potato mixture to the beaten eggs and then add the eggs to the soup. Remove from the heat, stir in the cheese, correct the seasoning, and serve at once.

Serves 6.

Pumpkin Soup with Münster Cheese and Cumin

Locro de Zapallo I

½ pound bacon, chopped

2 onions, chopped

4 pounds fresh pumpkin, peeled and cut into small pieces, or 1 can (29 ounces) unseasoned pumpkin purée

2 to 3 *serrano* or other medium-hot chilies, seeded and minced

2 teaspoons cumin seeds, ground

8 to 10 cups chicken stock

1 ½ cups grated Münster cheese

3 tablespoons chopped parsley

South American pumpkins are different from ours, being more like winter squash, which can be substituted. For this soup the squash are traditionally cooked in an earthenware casserole with salt and just enough water to prevent their burning. An ordinary soup kettle will do and, if time is scarce, canned pumpkin purée may be used. Fresh pumpkin contains considerably more moisture than does canned so adjust the amount of stock accordingly. If you prepare this locro *in advance, add the cheese just before re-heating the soup and serve it just as the cheese* begins *to melt.*

Cook the bacon until it is almost crisp. Add the onions and sauté them until they are very soft. Combine the bacon and onions with the pumpkin. Stir in the chiles and cumin and then add the stock until the soup reaches the desired consistency. Add the cheese and heat through but do not boil. Garnish with chopped parsley.

Serves 6.

Pumpkin Stew with Chilies and Cheese
Locro de Zapallo II

1 onion, coarsely chopped

2 cloves garlic, minced

2 to 4 *serrano* or *jalapeño* chilies, seeded and chopped

1 tablespoon safflower oil

2 pounds pumpkin (or winter squash) peeled and cut into 2-inch cubes

2 white potatoes, peeled and cut into eighths

¼ cup evaporated milk or half-and-half, at room temperature

1 cup white cheese (*queso blanco*) or *feta* cheese

Salt and pepper to taste

The sweet pumpkin and the slightly salty cheese provide an unexpected combination of flavors. Traditionally, this vegetarian stew is served with rice, but I prefer to serve a hearty lettuce and avocado salad. If the locro *is prepared ahead, add the cheese at the final heating.*

Sauté the onion, garlic and chilies in the oil. Add the pumpkin and potatoes and a little water, if necessary. Cover and cook over low heat until the pumpkin and potatoes are tender. Add the milk and cheese and heat through. Correct the seasoning. Garnish with additional cheese, if desired.

Serves 6.

Fish and Shellfish

Pescados y Mariscos, Peixe e mariscos

A glance at the map and it becomes clear that fish and shellfish are important components of South American cuisines. Along the west coast, the great Humboldt Current supplies Chile, Peru, and Ecuador with exceptional fish. Many of the varieties are unknown here but others available in our markets may be substituted, with no harm done to the dishes in the recipes that follow.

Besides the wonderful local bounty available to South Americans, many colonial descendants cherish a fondness for dried shrimp and dried salt cod. In Bahia especially, dried shrimp turn up in almost all the dishes for which the area is famous. For more information on dried shrimp, see page 18.

Fish Market, Santos, Brazil

Stuffed Striped Bass

Corvina Rellena

1 striped bass (3 to 4 pounds)

¼ cup lemon juice

1 teaspoon salt

Salt and pepper to taste

1 onion, finely chopped

3 cloves garlic, minced

6 to 8 green olives sliced

2 hard-boiled eggs, finely chopped

1 cup fresh bread crumbs

⅓ cup chopped cilantro

Milk

1 tablespoon butter

1 tablespoon olive oil

1 cup dry white wine

Have the fish cleaned and the bones removed (or do it yourself) but leave the head and tail intact. Soak the cleaned fish in lemon juice combined with 1 teaspoon salt for 1 hour, turning once.

Dry the fish, season it with salt and pepper inside and out if desired. Combine the onion, garlic, olives, hard-boiled eggs, bread crumbs, and cilantro. Moisten with enough milk to make a workable stuffing. Stuff the fish and fasten it together with toothpicks.

Place the fish in a buttered baking dish. Dot with butter, pour olive oil and wine over and bake in a pre-heated 400 degree oven for 12 minutes per pound (unstuffed weight).

Carefully, so as not to break the fish, remove it to a heated platter. Pour the pan juices over it and garnish, if desired, with sprigs of cilantro, lemon wedges, and sliced tomato.

Serves 4.

Bahian Seafood Stew
Vatapá de Camarão e Peixe

3 tablespoons safflower oil

1 teaspoon *dendê* oil, or substitute 1 additional tablespoon safflower oil

1 large onion, chopped

2 cloves garlic, minced

4 tomatoes, seeded, chopped

3 or 4 *habañero* chilies, chopped

Juice of one lemon

2 tablespoons chopped cilantro

Water

4 cups coconut milk

¼ cup dried shrimp, ground

½ cup roasted cashew nuts, ground

1 cup grated, unsweetened coconut

1 piece (1-inch) fresh ginger root, peeled and minced

1 pound raw shrimp, shelled and deveined

2 pounds bass or cod, cut into 4-inch pieces

Vatapá, *one of the African-inspired treasures of the Bahian cuisine, is an exotic combination of fish, fish and shrimp, chicken, or meat blended with dried shrimp, coconut milk, ground nuts,* dendê *oil, and many other ingredients. The final, wonderful blend of flavors is easier to enjoy than it is to identify. Modern appliances eliminate much of the tedious work that the dish once required and, despite the lengthy list of ingredients, it goes together quite quickly.*

Heat the safflower and *dendê* oils together and sauté the onion and garlic until the onion is soft. Add the tomatoes, chilies, lemon juice, cilantro, and a little water, if necessary, and simmer, stirring frequently, for 5 minutes. Add the coconut milk, the dried shrimp, and the cashews. Simmer for 2 to 3 minutes. Add the coconut and ginger and simmer for an additional 2 to 3 minutes.

Remove the sauce from the heat, pour it into a blender or food processor and purée until it is smooth. (If this is done in a blender, cool slightly before puréeing.) Return the puréed sauce to the pan and add a little water or coconut milk if it is too thick. Add the fish and shrimp, stir well to coat with the sauce and simmer just until the shrimp and fish are done, no more than 5 minutes. (If this dish is prepared ahead of time, it is important to add the fish and shrimp only at the final heating as they should not be overcooked.)

Serve the *vatapá* over rice and accompanied by two sauces: *Pirão de arroz* (page 170) and *Môlho de pimenta e limão* (page 171).

Serves 6.

Bahian Fish or Shrimp Stew
Moqueca de Camarão; Moqueca de Peixe

2 cloves garlic, pressed

2 pounds raw shrimp, peeled and deveined or 2 pounds firm white fish cut into large pieces

1 large onion, thinly sliced

2 or 3 *serrano* or *jalapeño* chilies, seeded and minced

Juice of 1 lemon

1 tablespoon chopped cilantro

2 tomatoes, peeled, seeded and chopped

1 ¼ cups coconut milk (page 16)

2 tablespoons *dendê* oil (see page 18), or 1 tablespoon *dendê* oil and 1 tablespoon olive oil

A moqueca *is a stewlike dish of fish or shellfish or a combination of the two. Sometimes it is made with chicken. The dish is a good example of the mingling that took place between the Indian and African cuisines in the kitchens of the Big Houses on the sugar plantations with results that are thoroughly Brazilian and particularly Bahian. Specifically,* moquecas *are the Africanized descendants of the native Indian* pokekas—*ragouts of fish and shellfish combined with oil and seasonings and originally wrapped in banana leaves and roasted over glowing coals. Today's stove-top cooking method is less quaint, but far easier, and the results do not suffer. Rice is the traditional accompaniment.*

Combine the garlic and shrimp or fish in a glass or stainless steel bowl and let them stand for 15 to 20 minutes.

Combine the onion, chilies, lemon juice, cilantro, tomatoes, and ¼ cup of the coconut milk and cook over low heat for 5 minutes. Add a little water, if necessary. Add the shrimp or fish, the olive oil and *dendê* to this mixture and continue to cook over low heat until the shrimp or the fish is cooked—about 3 to 5 minutes. Add the remaining cup of coconut milk and heat through. Do not overcook. Serve with *Farofa de azeite de dendê* (page 173).

Serves 6.

Chilean Fish Stew
Caldillo de Congrio

8 new potatoes, scrubbed, sliced ¼-inch thick

4 thick cod or bass steaks

Juice of one lemon

2 onions, thinly sliced

4 tomatoes, peeled, seeded, and coarsely chopped (optional)

2 cloves garlic, minced

1 small bay leaf

2 pieces lemon peel each 1-inch long

4 tablespoons chopped cilantro

½ teaspoon oregano

4 cups fish stock or 2 cups each clam juice and water

1 cup dry white wine

4 tablespoons olive oil

A caldillo is a light broth in Spain but this recipe is closer to a fish stew and, in Chile, congrio *is not an eel, despite the name, but a firm-fleshed fish, the pride of the Chilean waters. This fine fish is not available in the United States but either bass or cod are good substitutes. There are many versions of this recipe and, as is the case with our clam chowder, tomatoes are included if the cook wishes to do so.*

In a flameproof casserole large enough to hold all the ingredients, place a layer of sliced potatoes. Arrange the fish on top in a single layer and sprinkle with lemon juice. Continue to add potatoes, onions, tomatoes and garlic. Tuck in the bay leaf and lemon peel and sprinkle with cilantro and oregano. Add the fish stock and wine and, finally, drizzle the olive oil over all.

Bring to the boil on top of the stove. Immediately reduce the heat and simmer, partly covered, until the potatoes are done, about 20 minutes.

Serves 4.

Shrimp Stew or Chowder

Chupe de Camarón

6 green onions, including the green part, finely chopped

3 cloves garlic, minced

¼ cup safflower oil

3 tomatoes, peeled, seeded, and coarsely chopped

2 or 3 *serrano* or *jalapeño* chilies, seeded and finely chopped

½ teaspoon allspice

Salt and pepper to taste

3 quarts fish stock (or substitute chicken stock or part water and part clam juice)

2 potatoes, peeled and coarsely chopped

1 pound raw shrimp, peeled and deveined; reserve the shells

½ cup raw rice

3 medium potatoes, peeled and cut into quarters

2 cups peas (frozen are fine; canned are not)

2 ears corn, cut into 2-inch pieces

1 pound firm white fish fillets, cut into bite-sized pieces

3 eggs, lightly beaten

1 cup evaporated milk or half-and-half, at room temperature

3 tablespoons minced cilantro

Because it contains both milk and potatoes, we would probably call this dish a chowder. It is certainly in the same family and is exceptionally good so do not be put off by the long list of ingredients. Peru, Chile, and Ecuador each has many versions of this hearty meal in a soup plate and in Peru, it is almost a national dish. In one version the beaten eggs are omitted and instead, eggs are poached in the soup, one per person.

Sauté the onion and the garlic in the oil until the onion is soft. Add the tomatoes, chilies, allspice, and the salt and pepper and cook for 2 to 3 minutes, stirring well. Add the stock, the chopped potatoes, and the shrimp *shells* and bring the mixture to the boil. Reduce the heat, cover, and simmer for 30 minutes.

Strain the stock through a sieve, pressing hard to extract as much of the solids as possible, or run it through a food mill. Rinse the pan and return the stock.

Add the rice and the quartered potatoes, cover, and simmer until the potatoes and rice are done. Add the peas, corn, shrimp, and fish and simmer gently for 5 minutes. Do not boil or overcook at this point. With a fork, stir in the beaten eggs, allowing them to coagulate in threads. Add the milk and continue to simmer just long enough to heat through. Serve in soup plates garnished with minced cilantro.

Serves 6.

Fish Fillets with Shrimp Sauce
Efó

1 pound fresh shrimp or 2 cups dried shrimp

1 tablespoon safflower oil

2 or 3 *poblano* chilies, seeded and coarsely chopped

3 cloves garlic, chopped

1 onion, coarsely chopped

½ teaspoon coriander seeds, crushed

½ teaspoon oregano

1 pound spinach

¼ cup *dendê* oil (see page 18) (optional)

1 pound fish fillets (haddock, snapper, or bass)

This dish is one of the standards of the Bahian cuisine and, of course, there are many variations. I like to broil the fish fillets instead of sautéeing them, but either method may be used. I have discovered another use for the sauce; combined with hot cooked pasta, it makes a memorable meal.

Shell, devein, and clean the fresh shrimp or purée the dried shrimp in a blender. In a skillet, sauté the shrimp in the safflower oil with the chilies, garlic, onion, coriander seeds, and oregano for 2 to 3 minutes. Place the contents of the skillet in a blender or food processor and puré until smooth.

Wash the spinach and cook it in the water that clings to the leaves. When it is wilted, remove it from the heat and drain it very well. This is best accomplished by wringing it in a clean towel or pressing it in a potato ricer. Take the ball of squeezed spinach, slice it thinly and combine it with the shrimp purée. Add the *dendê* oil and heat the mixture just enough to melt the *dendê*.

Sauté the fish fillets in a small quantity of oil or butter, turning them once and cooking just until the fish flakes easily. Pour the sauce onto a hot platter and arrange the fish on top. Serve with *Pirão de arroz* (page 170).

Serves 4.

Fish Fillets in Sour Onion Sauce
Escabeche de Pescado

2 onions, thickly sliced

1 teaspoon dried *ancho* chilies, seeded and finely crushed

2 cloves garlic, pressed

2 to 3 tablespoons safflower oil

½ cup white wine vinegar

6 fish fillets (any firm-fleshed white fish)

Salt and pepper to taste

2 to 3 tablespoons flour

Lettuce leaves

2 avocados

Despite its name, this is not a true escabeche—*a pickled dish*—*but rather fish fillets in a sour onion sauce. The key to its success is to cook the sauce long enough (over low heat) for the onions to become very soft. The fish fillets may be broiled instead of sautéed if desired.*

Sauté the onion, chilies, and garlic in the oil over very low heat until the onions are very soft. Add the vinegar, cover, and immediately remove from the heat.

Dust the fillets with the combined salt, pepper, and flour. Sauté the fish quickly in hot oil, turning once to brown on both sides. Remove to a lettuce-lined platter. Mix the sauce well, pour over the fish, and garnish with sliced avocados.

Serves 6.

Fish in Peanut Sauce

Peixe com Môlho de Amendoim

6 pieces firm white fish, such as haddock or cod

3 tablespoons butter

2 onions, finely chopped

3 or 4 *serrano* or *jalapeño* chilies, seeded and minced

3 cloves garlic, minced

½ cup chicken stock

1 teaspoon coriander seed, crushed

One piece fresh ginger root, ½ an inch long, peeled and minced

¾ cup roasted peanuts, finely ground

Salt and pepper to taste

In Brazil, fish almost always comes to the table sauced in some way. This spicy peanut sauce is typical and is very good with most mild-flavored, firm-fleshed white fish. Traditional accompaniments are rice and fried bananas.

Dry the fish pieces with paper towels. Melt the butter in a large, heavy skillet and sauté the onion and chilies for 2 to 3 minutes. Add the garlic and the fish pieces and, over medium heat, brown the fish well on all sides.

Add the stock, coriander seed, ginger, and the ground peanuts. Simmer, uncovered, until the fish is just tender and flakes easily. The time will depend on the thickness of the fish pieces; probably about 10 minutes. Correct the seasoning and serve the fish with the sauce.

Serves 6.

Fish in Tangerine Sauce
Peixe com Môlho de Tangerina

1 whole sea bass or haddock (2 ½ to 3 pounds), or 2 pounds fillets

Salt and pepper to taste

1 teaspoon ground coriander seeds

3 tablespoons lemon juice

3 tablespoons safflower oil

2 tablespoons chopped cilantro

1 small red onion, thinly sliced and separated into rings

¾ cup dry white wine

¾ cup tangerine juice

This recipe may be made either with a whole fish or with fillets. The combination of flavors is excellent. For a more intense tangerine flavor, I sometimes use the undiluted, frozen, concentrated juice.

Season the fish with salt and pepper and sprinkle with lemon juice and coriander. Place it in a buttered, ovenproof casserole just large enough to hold it and drizzle it with the oil. Top with cilantro and onion rings and then pour the wine and tangerine juice over all.

Bake uncovered at 400 degrees for 25 to 30 minutes or until the fish flakes easily. Do not overcook. Garnish with additional cilantro, if desired.

Serves 4 to 6.

Salt Cod Pudding
Pudim de Bacalhau

4 tablespoons butter

2 tablespoons flour

2 ½ cups half-and-half

1 cup soft, fresh bread crumbs

1 ½ cups cooked salt cod, flaked (see page 18 for initial preparation)

6 eggs, separated

⅓ cup chopped parsley

Salt and pepper to taste

Although I am not particularly fond of dried salt cod, I do enthusiastically recommend this light pudding that is similar to a soufflé. It may also be baked in individual ramekins and will then, of course, require less time to set. I like to serve this Brazilian dish with a sauce from neighboring Colombia.

In a saucepan melt the butter and blend in the flour. With a wire whisk, blend in the half-and-half and cook over medium heat until the mixture thickens slightly. Stir in the bread crumbs and the salt cod. Beat the egg yolks lightly and add. Stir in the chopped parsley and salt and pepper. Remove from the heat and cool slightly.

Beat the egg whites until they hold soft peaks and fold them gently into the fish mixture. Pour into a buttered 6-cup ring mold or soufflé dish and bake at 350 degrees for 40 minutes or until the pudding is completely set. Unmold onto a hot platter or serve from the soufflé dish. Serve with Fresh Tomato and Cilantro Sauce (page 165).

Serves 6.

Squash and Shrimp Soufflé
Soufflé de Calabeza y Camarón

1 pound yellow or other summer squash

2 medium onions, minced

1 red or green bell pepper, seeded and minced

4 tablespoons butter

1 ½ tablespoons flour

⅔ cup milk

½ pound shrimp, peeled, cleaned, and chopped

Salt to taste

4 eggs, separated

Avocados

Cilantro

This well-seasoned soufflé is perfect for a light meal.

Scrub the squash, cut them into chunks, and cook until they are tender either in boiling water or by steaming. Drain, if cooked in water, and mash coarsely with a fork.

Sauté the onion and bell pepper in the butter until they are very soft. Add the flour and cook for 1 minute. Add the milk, stirring to blend well. Remove from the heat and transfer to a medium-sized bowl. Add the squash and shrimp, salt to taste, and stir in the lightly beaten egg yolks.

Beat the egg whites until they form soft peaks and fold them into the squash mixture. Pour the mixture into a 6-cup soufflé or straight-sided baking dish and bake it at 325 degrees for 25 to 30 minutes or until the soufflé is set and nicely brown on top. Garnish with sliced avocados and cilantro.

Serves 6.

Poultry

Aves

Chicken was unknown in South America before the Conquest, but today, because it is compatible with so many different ingredients and lends itself to almost as many preparations, it is no surprise to find chicken cooked with imagination and gusto all over the continent. Many of the preparations may at first reading seem unusual, but all are delicious, and the Bahian specialties, with their exotic blends of ingredients, are especially worth trying.

olive oil, egg, tomato and chicken

Batter-Fried Chicken
Pollo Rebozado

2 tablespoons yellow cornmeal

¼ cup milk

Salt and pepper to taste

2 eggs, lightly beaten

3 whole chicken breasts

5 tablespoons safflower oil

2 onions, coarsely chopped

4 cloves garlic, minced

6 tomatoes, peeled, seeded, and coarsely chopped

3 *ancho* or other mild dried chilies, seeded and crushed

⅓ cup chopped cilantro

1 teaspoon oregano

1 cup chicken stock

Although this dish is often prepared with a whole, cut-up chicken, it cooks more quickly and, I believe, becomes a more elegant entrée when small pieces of boned chicken breast are used instead.

Combine the cornmeal, milk, salt, pepper, and eggs and beat well.

Remove the skin and bones from the chicken and cut each breast into 3 or 4 pieces. Dry the chicken well.

Heat 2 tablespoons of the oil. Dip the chicken pieces into the cornmeal batter and sauté them quickly in the oil to brown on all sides. Remove the chicken to paper towels to drain.

Heat the remaining 3 tablespoons oil and sauté the onion until it is soft. Add the garlic, tomatoes, chilies, cilantro, oregano, and the chicken. Add the stock, bring it to a boil, reduce the heat, cover, and simmer until the chicken is fully cooked, but not overcooked, about 10 minutes.

Serves 6.

Chicken Chili

Ají de Gallina

½ cup safflower oil

3 onions, chopped

6 cloves garlic, minced

6 to 10 *jalapeño* or *habañero* chilies, liquidized in a blender

2 *jalapeño* chilies, seeded and minced

½ teaspoon allspice

1 tablespoon cumin seed, crushed

2 cups peanuts, roasted and coarsely chopped

½ cup freshly grated Parmesan cheese

1 chicken (3 ½ to 4 pounds), poached, meat removed from the bones, and cut up

¾ cup evaporated milk, at room temperature

Salt and pepper to taste

Accompaniments

6 small new potatoes, boiled

6 hard-boiled eggs, peeled and quartered

12 ripe olives

Peruvians, who relish their food well-seasoned with chilies, have a staggering number from which to choose. You can adjust the number in this, or any, recipe, to your taste. South Americans frequently use evaporated milk in their cooking. I usually substitute half-and-half and, in this recipe, I have sometimes improvised even further by using yogurt or sour cream with good results.

Heat the oil in a large saucepan and sauté the onion and garlic until the onion is soft. Add the chilies, both the liquidized and the minced, the allspice, cumin, peanuts, cheese, and the chicken meat and mix gently but thoroughly. Cook to heat through.

Two or three minutes before serving, stir in the milk and correct the seasoning. Serve garnished with boiled potatoes, hard-boiled eggs, and ripe olives.

Serves 6.

Drunken Chicken
Pollo Borracho

Half an onion, minced

4 cloves garlic, minced

2 tablespoons butter

⅓ pound diced ham

4 half chicken breasts, boned and skinned

½ teaspoon cumin seeds, crushed

½ teaspoon dried sage, crumbled

2 cups dry white wine

1 cup chicken stock

1 tablespoon flour (optional)

¼ cup capers, rinsed and drained

Drunken Chicken is popular throughout South America. I like to serve it at room temperature as a light entrée.

Sauté the onion and garlic in butter until the onion is soft.

Butter a heavy casserole large enough to hold all the ingredients. Place half of the ham in the bottom, the chicken breasts on top, and then the rest of the ham. Sprinkle with cumin and sage and add the sautéed onion and garlic. Add the wine and enough chicken stock to cover the chicken.

Cover the casserole and bake at 325 degrees for 15 to 20 minutes or until the chicken is done. It is important not to overcook the chicken lest it become dry.

Remove the chicken and ham to a deep, hot platter. Reduce the sauce over high heat, adding a tablespoon of flour mixed with water, if desired. Pour the sauce over the chicken and the ham. Sprinkle with capers.

Serves 4.

Chicken in Fruit Sauce
Galinha com Môlho de Frutas

Marinade (vinho d'alho)

2 cloves garlic

½ teaspoon salt

⅛ teaspoon pepper

¼ cup finely chopped celery

½ cup finely chopped onion

¼ cup minced parsley

¼ cup grated carrot

1 cup dry white wine

½ cup white wine vinegar

1 chicken (3½ to 4 pounds), cut into serving pieces or an equal quantity of chicken pieces

2 tablespoons butter

⅓ cup tomato sauce

½ cup orange juice

1 teaspoon grated orange peel

1 tablespoon lemon juice

½ teaspoon grated lemon peel

½ cup pitted dried prunes

½ cup pitted dates

¼ cup heavy cream

Brazilians serve this dish with coconut rice, but it is good with wild rice too. Although the dates and prunes are an unusually successful combination, don't hesitate to substitute or add other dried fruit and don't overlook Vinho d'alho *as a marinade for duck, turkey, and pork as well.*

To make the marinade, mash the garlic with the salt and pepper until it forms a smooth paste. Add the remaining ingredients and mix well.

Marinate the chicken pieces overnight or for at least 6 hours in the *Vinho d'alho*. Remove the chicken and reserve the marinade.

Brown the chicken on all sides in the butter. Gradually add the marinade. Then add the tomato sauce, orange juice, orange peel, lemon juice, lemon peel, the prunes, and the dates. Cover and simmer gently until the chicken is very tender, about 30 minutes. Add more orange juice if necessary.

When the chicken is done, remove it from the sauce, set it aside, and keep warm. Add the cream to the sauce and stir it quickly for several minutes to prevent its curdling. Pour the sauce over the chicken and serve at once.

Serves 4.

Pickled Chicken
Escabeche de Pollo

3 pounds chicken pieces (thighs are suitable), skin removed

3 small onions, quartered

3 carrots, scraped and sliced ¼-inch thick, diagonally

1 red or green bell pepper, seeded and sliced in rings

½ cup safflower oil

1 cup white wine vinegar

¼ cup water

½ teaspoon allspice

½ teaspoon oregano

1 bay leaf

1 piece cinnamon stick, 2-inches long

3 whole cloves

Salt and pepper to taste

Escabeche *dishes, which are popular throughout South America, are dishes in which the main ingredient (poultry, meat, or fish) is cooked and at the same time pickled in a sour, vinegar-based sauce. In this recipe, the natural gelatin in the chicken causes the sauce to set as it cools. It is especially delicious when served lightly chilled, at the point just before the jelly begins to soften and melt.*

Place all the ingredients in a pot large enough to hold them without crowding. Bring to a boil, skim off any foam, reduce the heat, cover, and simmer until the chicken is tender, about 45 minutes.

Transfer the contents of the pot to an attractive serving dish and chill. The broth will set as it cools and provide a well-flavored jelly for the chicken and vegetables.

Serves 6.

Chicken in Shrimp and Nut Sauce
Xin-Xin de Galinha

1 chicken (3 ½ to 4 pounds),
cut into serving pieces

4 tablespoons lemon juice

¼ cup *dendê* oil (see page 18)
or ¼ cup safflower oil

¼ cup dried shrimp

2 cloves garlic, minced

1 onion, finely chopped

2 teaspoons ground coriander
seed

2 *habañero* chilies, seeded and
minced

½ cup roasted peanuts, ground

1 cup chicken stock

Chopped parsley

Chopped fresh mint

This great Bahian dish has many variations but it always includes chicken, dried shrimp, dendê *oil, and ground nuts—"basic" ingredients that never fail to produce an exotically seasoned bird. If* dendê *oil is unavailable, the end result will not suffer greatly from the omission.*

Sprinkle the chicken with lemon juice and set aside.

Heat the oil and sauté the dried shrimp, garlic, onion, coriander, and chiles for 2 to 3 minutes. Add the peanuts and the stock and stir well. Add the chicken, cover, and simmer until the chicken is done.

The sauce should be thick and coat the chicken well. If it is too thin, remove the chicken when it is done, reduce the sauce to the proper consistency, and return the chicken to the sauce. Correct the seasoning. Garnish with chopped parsley and/or mint and serve with rice.

Serves 6.

Chicken Stew Bahian-Style
Vatapá de Galinha

1 onion, sliced

3 cloves garlic, minced

2 to 4 *habañero* or *jalapeño* chilies, seeded and chopped

¼ cup chopped cilantro

3 tomatoes, peeled, seeded, and chopped

2 tablespoons olive oil

1 chicken (2 ½ to 3 pounds), cut up, or an equivalent quantity of chicken pieces

Chicken stock as necessary

2 cups coconut milk (page 16)

1 cup dried shrimp, finely ground (page 18)

1 cup roasted peanuts, ground

Salt and pepper to taste

2 tablespoons *dendê* oil (optional) (page 18)

Preparing and eating a vatapá, *with its subtle blend of flavors, is almost the next best thing to being in Bahia. Because I do not care for dried shrimp, I use far less than this recipe calls for without, I believe, adversely affecting the final result. If you choose to experiment, the license is yours because this is a dish of infinite variation.*

Sauté the onion, garlic, chilies, cilantro and tomatoes in the olive oil until the mixture is thick and soft. This mixture is called a *refogado* and comprises the first step in many Brazilian dishes. Add the chicken pieces and stir in a little chicken stock if the mixture is too dry. Simmer gently until the chicken is very tender.

Remove the chicken, take the meat off the bones, and set it aside. Combine the sauce in which the chicken was cooked, with the coconut milk, dried shrimp, and the ground peanuts. Heat this mixture slowly. It should be the consistency of a thick *béchamel* sauce, so add a little more stock, if necessary. Stir in the *dendê* oil and then the chicken. Heat through.

Serve with *Pirão de arroz* (page 169) and *Farofa de azeite de dendê* (page 173).

Serves 6.

Corn Pie with Chicken
Pastel de Choclo con Relleno de Pollo

1 chicken (3 ½ to 4 pounds)

⅓ cup raisins

2 onions, chopped

3 tablespoons safflower oil

3 tomatoes, peeled, seeded, and chopped

½ teaspoon cinnamon

2 hard-boiled eggs, chopped

3 cloves garlic, minced

3 *poblano* chilies, seeded and chopped

Salt and pepper to taste

¼ cup chopped parsley

Pie Crust

½ cup butter

4 cups corn kernels (frozen are preferable to canned)

⅓ cup chopped cilantro

2 teaspoons sugar

4 eggs

Salt to taste

Paprika for dusting

This deliciously seasoned dish is excellent when prepared according to the recipe below and equally good if pork or beef are substituted for the chicken. The chicken mixture alone makes an unusual salad that is especially good when paired with avocados and fresh fruit. The corn mixture alone can be used as a vegetable or a side dish. All in all, this is a versatile recipe.

Simmer the chicken in water to cover until it is very tender. Remove the meat, discarding the skin and bones. Cut the meat into bite-sized pieces and set aside.

Soak the raisins in warm water for 5 minutes. Drain and set aside.

Sauté the onion in the oil until it is soft. Add the tomatoes, raisins, cinnamon, eggs, garlic, and chilies and cook for 2 minutes. Stir in the chicken and the parsley, remove from the heat, and set aside.

To make the pie crust, melt the butter in a saucepan large enough to hold the rest of the ingredients. Purée the corn in a blender or food processor and add to the melted butter. Add the cilantro and sugar and cook over very low heat for 2 to 3 minutes. Add the eggs one at a time and mix well. Add salt. Cook and stir until the mixture thickens, then cool to room temperature.

Butter a 2-quart casserole and, using about two-thirds of the corn mixture, line the bottom and sides of the dish. Carefully, add the chicken and top it with the remaining corn. Dust the top with paprika. Bake at 350 degrees for about 1 hour or until the topping is set and nicely browned.

Serves 6.

Couscous with Chicken
Cuscuz de Galinha

Chicken and Sauce

Juice of 1 lemon

½ teaspoon grated lemon peel

1 onion, chopped fine

2 cloves garlic, pressed

Salt and pepper to taste

1 teaspoon ground coriander

2 tablespoons safflower oil

¼ cup white wine vinegar

½ cup tomato sauce

½ cup water

1 frying chicken, cut up, or an equal amount of chicken pieces

Cornmeal cuscuz

4 cups white cornmeal

1 cup butter

1 cup salted, boiling water

This is one of many Brazilian versions of couscous. *From its ancient Arabian origins and its more recent North African heritage,* cuscuz *is firmly entrenched in the Brazilian cuisine. That it is made from cornmeal rather than wheat seems appropriate to the New World. Pieces of chicken, meat, or seafood, hard-boiled eggs, olives, and vegetables are added and the whole is steamed in a special utensil called a* cuscuzeiro.

Without an authentic *cuscuzeiro*, you will need to improvise. A colander placed inside a large pan that has a tight-fitting lid is quite satisfactory. A large pot with a round-bottomed steamer-basked insert is an almost perfect substitute.

The unmolded result is an aromatic and beautiful dome studded with vegetables and meat. Although it is not difficult, time and patience are required to prepare a *cuscuz*. It is worth the effort.

To prepare the chicken, combine the lemon juice and peel, onion, garlic, salt and pepper, coriander, oil, vinegar, tomato sauce and water in a heavy pan. Add the chicken pieces, cover, and cook over medium heat until the chicken is tender, 1 to 1 ½ hours. Remove the chicken from the sauce and, when cool enough to handle, bone it, and discard the skin and bones. Reserve 1 ½ cups of the sauce.

To prepare the cornmeal *cuscuz*, heat the cornmeal in a heavy skillet over medium heat. Stir occasionally and watch carefully. When it just begins to turn pale brown (this takes about 5 minutes), remove it from the heat. Melt the butter in the water and when it is melted, add the mixture to the cornmeal. Return the skillet to the heat and stir for 2 minutes to combine well.

Cuscuz

1 cut-up, boned chicken (see above)

1 ½ cups chicken cooking sauce (see above)

2 to 3 *serrano* or *jalapeño* chilies, seeded and finely chopped

½ cup melted butter

¼ cup chopped cilantro

Cornmeal "couscous" (see above)

⅓ pound cooked ham, diced

6 cherry tomatoes, cut in half

2 cups frozen peas

3 hard-boiled eggs, sliced

12 to 15 pimiento stuffed olives

Orange slices

To assemble the *cuscuz*: Heat the chicken and the sauce together. Add the chilies, butter, cilantro, and salt and pepper. Remove from the heat and slowly stir in the prepared cornmeal. Mix well and add the ham. Test a pinch of the mixture to see if it will form a ball and hold its shape. If is too dry, add a little water.

Lightly oil a 3-quart colander. Place sliced tomatoes, eggs, and olives in rows on the bottom and up the sides of the colander, helping them to adhere with a little of the cornmeal mixture. Add more cornmeal, pressing it firmly but gently to the bottom and sides, Add layers of peas, eggs, tomatoes, and olives alternately with cornmeal until all of the ingredients are used.

Cover the colander with a cloth napkin or a folded tea towel. Steam until the napkin is very wet, about 1 hour. The time will depend on the size of the colander. *Be careful that the water does not reach the level of the colander bottom and that the water does not evaporate completely.*

When it is done, let the *cuscuz* stand for 5 minutes before unmolding it onto a hot serving platter. Garnish it with parsley or cilantro springs, if desired and serve with a generous plate of sliced oranges.

Serves 8 to 10.

Duck and Rice Cooked in Beer
Arroz con Pato

1 duck (4 to 5 pounds), cut into serving pieces

1 tablespoon safflower oil

1 large onion, thickly sliced

2 pieces lemon peel, each about 1-inch long

3 cloves garlic, minced

1 teaspoon cumin seeds, crushed

Salt and pepper to taste

¾ cup chopped cilantro

3 cups chicken stock

3 cups beer

2 cups raw long-grained rice

¾ cup chopped cilantro

Chicken with Rice (Arroz con pollo) is popular throughout most of South America but Peruvians often prefer duck instead of chicken with their rice.

Prick the duck skin all over with a fork. Heat the oil in a large, heavy casserole; add the duck and the onions, and sauté over medium-high heat until the duck pieces are nicely browned on all sides and the onions are golden. Drain off the fat.

Add the lemon peel, garlic, cumin, salt and pepper, cilantro, chicken stock, and beer to the casserole. Bring the liquid to the boil, lower the heat, and simmer, covered, until the duck is very tender, about 45 minutes. Remove the duck to a hot platter and keep warm.

Drain off the liquid and measure 3 ½ cups. Add the rice to the casserole with the measured cooking liquid. Cover and cook until the rice is tender and has absorbed all the liquid, about 20 minutes. Serve the duck and rice together on a platter. Garnish with additional cilantro.

Serves 4 to 6.

Marinated Turkey Casserole
Cazuela de Pavo

Marinade

3 cloves garlic, minced

1 teaspoon salt

Freshly ground black pepper to taste

1 ½ cups dry white wine

1 ½ cups orange juice

Half a turkey breast (approximately 2 ½ to 3 pounds), or other turkey parts

1 tablespoon butter

1 tablespoon safflower oil

2 medium onions, thickly sliced

4 tomatoes, peeled, seeded, and coarsely chopped

1 bay leaf

2 or 3 *jalapeño* or *serrano* chilies, seeded and thinly sliced

⅔ cup toasted cashew nuts, ground or finely chopped

I like the unusual blend of flavors in this simple casserole. Try using the same marinade for chicken or for a pork loin roast. In both cases, cooking times will need to be adjusted.

To make the marinade, combine the garlic, salt, pepper, wine, and orange juice in a shallow dish. Add the turkey, cover, and refrigerate overnight or for at least 6 hours. Turn the turkey in the marinade several times.

Remove the turkey and reserve the marinade. In a heavy casserole, sauté the turkey in the butter and oil until it is nicely browned on all sides. Add the onions, tomatoes, bay leaf, chilies, and the reserved marinade. Cover and bake at 350 degrees for 30 minutes. Stir in the cashew nuts and continue to bake, uncovered, for an additional 30 minutes or until the meat is tender. Correct the seasoning. If a thicker sauce is desired, remove the cooked turkey and reduce the marinade over high heat.

Slice the turkey on a platter and pass the sauce separately.

Serves 4.

Meat

Carne

A good many of the meat dishes that I have included in this section combine relatively inexpensive cuts of meat with fairly long lists of ingredients and a wide range of sometimes unusual seasonings. The South American penchant for combining meat with fruit is a legacy from the Spanish and Portuguese colonizers who learned the techniques during the long Moorish occupation. It is surprising, however, how few New World fruits have invaded the repertoire.

Most of these dishes are ideal for informal gatherings and several, as noted, provide interesting party entrées. *Feijoada* is a party in itself and well worth the effort.

Meat Market, Santos, Brazil

Beef Stew with Dried Fruit

Cocido de Fruta Paso

1½ cups pitted, mixed dried fruit (prunes, pears, peaches, apricots)

3 tablespoons raisins

3 pounds top round, cut into thin strips

3 tablespoons safflower oil

1 onion, finely chopped

2 cloves garlic, minced

1 carrot, scrubbed and coarsely chopped

1 red or green bell pepper, seeded and coarsely chopped

1 piece cinnamon stick, about 2-inches long

1 teaspoon oregano, crushed

1 cup dry red wine

The origins of this popular stew lie in the Middle East where dried fruit and meat cooked together are a time-honored combination. It makes a wonderful meal. I sometimes add a pared, sliced apple or two during the last five minutes of cooking. This is not strictly authentic, but very good just the same.

Soak the dried fruit and the raisins in 1½ cups warm water for 30 minutes. Drain and reserve the soaking liquid.

Sauté the beef in the oil in a heavy ovenproof casserole. Add the onion, garlic, carrot, bell pepper, cinnamon stick and the oregano and cook over medium heat for 5 minutes. Add the wine and the reserved soaking liquid. Cover and bake at 325 degrees for 1 hour. Add more water while cooking, if necessary. Add the dried fruit, either cut up or whole depending on the size, and the raisins. Return the casserole to the oven for an additional 20 minutes.

Serve with rice.

Serves 6.

Beefsteak in the Style of Montevideo
Biftik à la Montevideo

3 onions; 1 chopped, 2 sliced thickly

3 cloves garlic, minced

4 tablespoons safflower oil

2 to 4 *jalapeño* or *serrano* chilies, seeded and chopped

2 pounds round steak or London broil, well trimmed

Salt and pepper to taste

3 tomatoes, peeled, seeded, and thickly sliced

1 to 2 tablespoons flour

¾ cup beef broth

This is not fancy fare but it is nicely seasoned and just plain good eating.

Sauté the chopped onion and the garlic in the oil until the onion is soft. Add the chilies and sauté for an additional 3 or 4 minutes. With a slotted spoon, remove most of the onion and chilies and reserve them.

Rub the steak with salt and pepper and sauté it in the same pan. Brown it well on both sides.

Place a layer of the sliced onions in the bottom of an ovenproof casserole that is not much larger than the steak. Place the meat on top of the onions, cover it with the remaining onions, and season with salt and pepper. Cover the casserole and bake at 350 degrees until the meat is almost tender. The time will depend on the meat but it will probably be about an hour.

Add the tomatoes and continue to bake until the meat is very tender.

In a separate pan combine 1 tablespoon of the flour with ¼ cup of the beef broth and whisk until it is smooth. Gradually whisk in the remaining broth and add the reserved onion and chilies. Correct the seasoning.

Remove the steak to a deep platter, slice it thinly across the grain, and pour the gravy over.

Serves 4.

Beef Pie with Peaches or Apricots
Pastel de Carne y Durazno ó Albaricoque

Filling

2 ½ pounds beef sirloin, well-trimmed and very thinly sliced

2 tablespoons safflower oil

2 onions, thinly sliced

½ cup dry white wine

¼ cup sugar

1 teaspoon oregano

1 teaspoon cinnamon

½ teaspoon ground cloves

½ teaspoon allspice

1 small bay leaf

Salt and pepper to taste

⅔ cup raisins, soaked in warm water

6 fresh peaches, peeled, pitted, and halved or 24 canned apricot halves, well drained

Pastry

3 cups flour

⅓ cup sugar

½ pound butter, cut into pieces

3 egg yolks

2 to 4 tablespoons dry white wine

To my mind, this is a perfect party dish, unusual, showy, and utterly delicious. It is also a perfect example of the Argentine skill in combining meat and fruit. If good fresh peaches are not available, I have found that canned and well-drained apricot halves are the best substitute. Canned peaches are too sweet for this dish, which already has more than a hint of sweetness.

To make the filling, place the meat in the freezer for 30 minutes to make it easier to slice. After slicing, pat it dry with paper towels and sauté it quickly in hot oil to brown lightly. Add the onions, lower the heat, cook and stir until the onions are soft. Add the wine, sugar, oregano, cinnamon, cloves, allspice, bay leaf, and salt and pepper. Bring the mixture to the boil, reduce the heat, cover, and simmer gently for 15 minutes. Drain the raisins and add them to the meat. Remove the bay leaf. Transfer the filling to a shallow bowl to cool to room temperature.

To make the pastry, combine the flour, sugar, and butter with a pastry blender or process in a food processor until the mixture resembles coarse cornmeal. Add the egg yolks one at a time and then the wine very slowly, using only enough to form a soft dough.

Divide the dough in half and refrigerate both pieces until they are thoroughly chilled—at least 30 minutes.

When properly chilled, take one piece from the refrigerator and roll the dough on a lightly floured board until it is about 4 inches larger than the dish you plan to use. A 9- by 13- by 2-inch baking dish is a good size. The crust should be about ⅛-inch thick.

To assemble the pie, place the dough loosely over the dish and press it gently to the bottom and along the sides. Add the meat filling and spread it evenly. Top the meat with the peach or apricot halves, cut-side down. Cover them with the second piece of pastry, also rolled ⅛-inch thick. The top crust should sink into the dish slightly. Seal the edges with the tines of a fork and cut off the excess dough.

Meringue

4 egg whites

1 tablespoon sugar

Bake the pie at 375 degrees for 30 minutes or until the crust is nicely browned. Remove it from the oven and set the oven to broil.

To make the meringue, beat the egg whites until they form soft peaks. Add the sugar and continue beating until the meringue is firm and glossy. Spread it over the top of the pie and place the pie 3 inches below the broiler. Cook just until the top is lightly browned. Watch carefully. Serve at once.

Serves 6.

Corn Pie with Meat and Chicken
Pastel de Carne y Pollo

2 pounds lean ground round

3 tablespoons safflower oil

3 cups coarsely chopped onion

3 cloves garlic, minced

½ cup raisins, soaked in warm water to cover

3 to 4 dried *ancho* or other mild dried chilies, seeds removed and finely crumbled

4 teaspoons cumin seeds, ground

1 teaspoon oregano

Salt and pepper to taste

⅔ cup pitted black olives, sliced

3 cups cooked chicken, shredded

6 cups corn kernels (frozen corn is acceptable)

⅓ cup milk

1 teaspoon sugar

I like to serve this generous dish at an informal gathering. The meat is flavored in a typically South American style with a pleasing combination of sweet raisins, hot peppers, and mild olives. If it is baked in a wide, shallow container (a 9- by 13- by 2-inch dish, for example), it may be necessary to increase the amount of corn topping because it is important to have a good thick layer so that it drizzles down into the chicken. This recipe can be easily doubled or tripled and the corn topping by itself makes a delightful side dish.

Brown the meat in 2 tablespoons of the oil in a large, heavy skillet. Stir in the onions, garlic, well-drained raisins, chili peppers, cumin, and oregano. Add salt and pepper. Reduce the heat and cook over low heat, uncovered, for 20 minutes. Stir occasionally. Drain any excess liquid, add the olives, and transfer the mixture to a shallow 2-quart casserole. Spread the chicken on top of the meat.

In a blender or food processor purée the corn with the milk. Heat 1 tablespoon of the oil in a heavy skillet and add the corn purée. Cook, stirring constantly, over medium heat until the mixture becomes quite thick. This should take about 5 minutes, but stir and watch carefully as it burns easily. When thick, pour the corn mixture over the chicken layer, spreading it evenly to the edges of the casserole. Sprinkle the top with sugar.

Bake at 350 degrees for 30 minutes. Then place it under the broiler just long enough to brown the top nicely.

Serves 6.

Creole Flag—Flank Steak with Black Beans and Rice
Pabellón Criollo

1½ to 2 pounds flank steak, cut into 3 or 4 pieces

1 bay leaf

Beef stock to cover

2 tablespoons olive oil

1 onion, coarsely chopped

2 cloves garlic, minced

4 tomatoes, peeled, seeded, and coarsely chopped

Salt and pepper to taste

½ teaspoon cumin seeds, crushed

1 teaspoon oregano

Arroz blanco (White Rice, page 157)

Caraotas negras (Black Beans, page 139)

2 very firm bananas

2 tablespoons safflower oil

Pabellón *means "flag" and a Venezuelan flag is what this dish resembles when it is properly set forth. Three of the main ingredients, black beans, rice, and flank steak, are dear to the hearts of Venezuelans. In fact, this is something of a national dish in that country. The final presentation is as attractive as it is good to eat.*

Simmer the meat and the bay leaf in the stock for 1 to 1½ hours or until the meat is very tender. Allow it to cool in the stock. When it is completely cool, remove the meat from the stock, shred it, and set it aside.

In the olive oil, sauté the onion until it is soft. Add the garlic, tomatoes, salt, pepper, cumin, and oregano and continue to cook over low heat until the mixture is quite dry. Add the shredded meat and correct the seasoning.

Cut the bananas into 3-inch pieces and sauté them in the safflower oil over medium heat until they are lightly browned all over. Drain them on paper towels.

To assemble the "flag," arrange the beef, rice, and beans on a rectangular platter in three rows with the rice in the center. Garnish with the sautéed bananas. In some recipes, the meat is further embellished by a topping of fried eggs—one per person—but the dish is substantial enough without that last minute addition.

Serves 6.

Stuffed Flank Steak
Matambre

1 flank steak, 3 to 4 pounds

Marinade

½ cup red wine vinegar

¼ cup olive or safflower oil

Salt and pepper to taste

1 teaspoon oregano

2 teaspoons chopped parsley

1 teaspoon cumin seeds, crushed

2 cloves garlic, pressed

Filling

1 small bunch spinach, cleaned and stems removed

3 small carrots, peeled, halved lengthwise, and parboiled until flexible

2 hard-boiled eggs, quartered lengthwise

1 small onion, sliced and separated into rings

3 cloves garlic, sliced

1 teaspoon oregano

1 tablespoon cumin seeds, crushed

Salt, pepper, and paprika to taste

String

Beef broth to cover

Salsa criolla (page 164)

Matambre means "kill hunger" from the Spanish words matar, *to kill, and* el hambre, *hunger. This is a popular dish throughout South America where it is served either hot or cold, as a first course or as an entrée. With all the good things rolled up inside, it is very attractive when sliced. The larger the piece of meat, the easier it is to roll.*

Trim any fat or gristle from the meat, split it horizontally, and pound it gently with a smooth-ended mallet to flatten it evenly.

To make the marinade, combine the ingredients and pour it over the meat in a shallow glass dish. Allow the meat to marinate for 4 to 5 hours at room temperature or overnight in the refrigerator.

To assemble, remove the meat from the marinade and place it on a flat surface. Cover it with two layers of spinach leaves. Arrange the carrots across the meat with the eggs in between. Cover these with a layer of onion rings and sprinkle with sliced garlic, oregano, cumin, salt, pepper and paprika.

Carefully roll the meat jelly-roll fashion and tie it with a string at 1-inch intervals. Place the roll in a fairly close-fitting ovenproof casserole and cover it with beef stock. Cover the casserole and bake at 350 degrees for 1½ to 2 hours.

If the *matambre* is to be served hot, remove it to a hot platter when done and allow it to rest for 10 to 15 minutes. Carefully remove the string and slice the roll in ¾-inch slices with a *very* sharp knife. Serve with *Salsa criolla*.

If it is to be served cold, let the meat cool in the broth. Then remove it to a shallow dish. Put a plate on top of it and on top of that a heavy can. Refrigerate the meat overnight or at least for several hours. Carefully remove the string and slice it in ¾-inch slices with a *very* sharp knife. Serve with *Salsa criolla*.

Serves 6 to 8.

Old Clothes—Spicy Shredded Meat
Roupa Velha; Ropa Vieja

1½ pounds flank steak

1 onion, chopped

3 cloves garlic, minced

4 to 6 *jalapeño* or *serrano* chilies, seeded and chopped

2 tablespoons safflower oil

3 tomatoes, peeled, seeded, and chopped

1 teaspoon oregano

1 teaspoon cumin seed, crushed

Salt and pepper to taste

Roupa velha *(in Portuguese)*, Ropa vieja *(in Spanish) are the names of a popular dish with almost as many variations as there are cooks. The same dish is also popular in both Portugal and Spain and the name means "old clothes." It is frequently, but not always, made from leftover meat. The one requirement is that the meat or fowl should be stringy to resemble rags or old clothes. In Brazil, dried beef, left over from making* feijoada, *is often used.*

If, as in this recipe, the dish is prepared from scratch, flank steak is a good choice because it shreds well. Traditionally, Roupa velha *is served as an entrée with rice, but it also makes a tasty sandwich filling, especially with pita bread.*

Poach the meat until it is tender, cool, and pull it into shreds. There should be approximately 3 cups of meat.

Sauté the onion, garlic, and chili peppers in the oil until the onion is soft. Add the tomatoes, oregano, and cumin. Stir and cook until the sauce is smooth and thick. Add the meat and salt and pepper. Simmer for a few minutes, adding a little water, if necessary.

Serves 4.

Creole Stew of Many Flavors
Carbonada Criolla

3 tablespoons safflower oil

2 pounds lean beef (such as top round), cut into 1-inch cubes

1 onion, coarsely chopped

1 red or green bell pepper, seeded and coarsely chopped

2 *jalapeño* or *serrano* chilies, seeded and finely chopped

4 cloves garlic, minced

2 tomatoes, peeled, seeded, and chopped

1 *bouquet garni* (parsley, bay leaf, thyme, oregano)

Salt and pepper to taste

4 to 5 cups beef stock

1 medium sweet potato, peeled and cubed

1 medium white potato, peeled and cubed

1 cup pre-soaked white pea beans

2 tart apples, peeled, cored, and diced

2 small zucchini, cut in 1-inch slices

2 ears of corn, cut in 2-inch slices

12 dried apricots

Even though Carbonada criolla *is one of Argentina's classic creole dishes, it is difficult to find two recipes that agree on every detail because enterprising cooks often include whatever is on hand.* Carbonada *is an interesting blend of* many *flavors—definitely a real meal for hungry people.*

Without a great deal of extra work, the carbonada *can be served from a pumpkin shell (it is then called* en calabeza*), a neat trick that almost automatically transforms it into a festive dish. To make a pumpkin shell container, select a nicely shaped, 10- to 12-pound pumpkin. Scrub it well and cut off a "lid" about one quarter of the way down. Keep the stem on the lid to use as a handle. With a metal spoon, thoroughly clean out the seeds and stringy fibers from inside the pumpkin. Pat it dry with a paper towel and rub the inside lightly with soft butter. Replace the lid. Place the pumpkin on a cookie sheet and bake it at 350 degrees for about 45 minutes. Check frequently after 30 minutes because it will collapse if overcooked. It should be tender when pierced with a sharp knife point but still firm enough to hold its shape. When done, set the pumpkin shell on a serving platter and fill it with the* carbonada.

To make the *carbonada*, heat the oil in a heavy flame-proof casserole. Add the meat and brown it well over medium heat. Add the onion, bell pepper, chilies, garlic and tomatoes and cook until the onion is soft. Add the *bouquet garni*, salt and pepper, stock, the sweet and white potatoes, and the beans.

Cover, reduce the heat, and simmer until the meat, potatoes, and beans are tender. Check during cooking and add more stock if necessary. Add the apples, zucchini, corn, and apricots and cook for an additional 5 minutes. Remove the *bouquet garni* and serve from the casserole or from a prepared pumpkin shell.

Serves 6.

Lamb Stew with Sweet Spices
Cazuela de Cordero

2 tablespoons safflower oil

2 pounds lamb shoulder, boned, well-trimmed, and cubed

2 onions, thinly sliced

2 cloves garlic, minced

Salt and pepper to taste

1 cup chicken stock

6 whole cloves

2 pieces cinnamon stick, each about 1-inch long

1 piece fresh ginger root (about 1-inch long), peeled and minced

2 tablespoons lemon juice

½ cup cream, at room temperature

Minced parsley

The Middle Eastern heritage of the Spanish conquerors shows up again in the seasonings of this somewhat exotic and well-flavored stew. Serve it with rice or some other starch as the sauce is quite liquid. If you make it ahead, add the cream at the final reheating.

Heat the oil in a heavy casserole and sauté the lamb, onions, and garlic until the meat is browned and the onions are soft. Add the salt, pepper, stock, cloves, cinnamon, and ginger.

Cover, reduce the heat, and simmer for 30 minutes. Add the lemon juice and continue to cook until the meat is fork-tender.

Just before serving, add the cream. Stir to combine but do not allow the sauce to boil. Garnish with minced parsley.

Serves 6.

Pork with Fruit and Almonds
Cerdo con Frutas

6 thick, meaty pork chops

2 tablespoons butter

2 tablespoons safflower oil

1 cup dried apricots

¾ cup golden raisins

½ cup roasted almonds, ground

3 cups orange juice

1 teaspoon grated orange peel

1 piece fresh ginger root 1-inch long, peeled and minced

1 piece cinnamon stick, about 2-inches long

½ teaspoon freshly ground nutmeg

½ teaspoon allspice

1 avocado, peeled and sliced

As this dish bakes, the aroma is simply captivating. It is another example of the South American cook's skill in combining meat and fruit, a combination I find always delicious.

Trim most of the fat from the pork chops. Melt the butter with the oil in a heavy casserole large enough to hold all the ingredients. Brown the chops quickly on both sides. Add all the other ingredients except the avocado. Cover the casserole and bake at 300 degrees for an hour or until the meat is tender and well cooked.

Remove the chops to a hot platter and keep warm. Discard the cinnamon stick. Correct the seasoning of the pan juices and reduce them over high heat to the consistency of gravy. Serve the juices with the chops and garnish with slices of avocado.

Serves 6.

Pork Hash
Picadinho de Porco

1 large onion, finely chopped

2 tablespoons butter

3 tomatoes, peeled, seeded, and chopped

3 to 4 *jalapeño* or *serrano* chilies, seeded and minced

2 cloves garlic, minced

½ teaspoon sage leaves, crumbled

¾ pound well-seasoned bulk pork sausage

2 pounds lean pork, ground

4 tablespoons lemon juice

Salt and pepper to taste

2 hard-boiled eggs, chopped

12 pitted ripe olives, halved

Picadinho *in Portuguese or* picadillo *in Spanish is generally translated as "hash." Probably more accurate is "minced meat" but whatever the definition, the results are almost always good. I've found a number of uses for this zesty Brazilian version in addition to its usual one as an entrée. It makes a perfect filling for* empanadas *and an excellent stuffing for vegetables such as onions, zucchini, or* chayote. *If you are really feeling adventurous, try it for breakfast topped with a fried or poached egg.*

Sauté the onion in butter until it is soft. Add the tomatoes, chilies, garlic, and sage. Mix well and simmer gently until the mixture thickens. Add the sausage and the ground pork and break up the meat so that it cooks and browns well. Simmer the mixture gently, stirring occasionally, for 15 to 20 minutes. Add the lemon juice and correct the seasoning.

If the *Picadinho* is to be served as an entrée, pile it onto a platter and top it with the chopped hard-boiled eggs and the olives. If it is to be used as a filling, add the eggs and the olives after it has cooled slightly. Stir gently to combine.

Serves 6 as an entrée.

Tomatillos

Pork with Lemon
Cerdo con Limon

2 pounds boneless pork butt or shoulder, trimmed of fat

2 tablespoons flour

¼ cup safflower oil

1 tablespoon peeled and minced ginger root

1 large onion, thinly sliced

3 tomatoes, peeled, seeded, and chopped

3 to 4 *jalapeño* or *serrano* chilies, seeded and minced

2 tablespoons minced parsley

½ teaspoon finely grated lemon peel

½ cup lemon juice

2 cups chicken stock

Lemon wedges

Chopped parsley

In South America, pork is almost always cooked with lemon juice and then served with more lemon. This very flavorful stewlike dish should be served with rice or potatoes.

Cut the pork into 1-inch cubes and sprinkle with flour. Heat the oil and sauté the meat with the ginger until the pork is nicely browned on all sides. Add the onion, tomatoes, and chilies and cook for 2 to 3 minutes. Add the parsley, lemon peel, lemon juice, and the stock.

Reduce the heat and simmer, uncovered, until the meat is fork-tender and the stock is reduced to the consistency of gravy. Serve the meat garnished with lemon wedges and chopped parsley.

Serves 6.

Roast Loin of Pork with Raisins
Costillar de Cerdo Asado a la Pasas

1 cup sweet vermouth or sweet white wine

¼ teaspoon anise seeds, crushed

½ teaspoon ground cloves

½ teaspoon allspice

1 piece fresh ginger root (about 1-inch long), peeled and minced

⅓ cup light brown sugar

3 pounds loin of pork

½ cup fine dry bread crumbs

6 tablespoons butter

1 cup milk

½ teaspoon cinnamon

1 cup golden raisins

Loin of pork has never tasted better. The seasonings are sweet and spicy and the aroma is wonderful while it cooks. I like to keep the rest of the meal simple: apple soup, buttered noodles, and steamed or quickly sautéed vegetables.

Combine the vermouth, anise seeds, cloves, allspice, ginger, and brown sugar in a baking dish. Add the pork and turn to coat it on all sides. Refrigerate overnight, turning once or twice if possible.

Sprinkle the meat with bread crumbs and dot with 3 tablespoons of the butter. Combine the remaining butter, milk, cinnamon and raisins and add this mixture to the marinade in the baking dish. Bake at 325 degrees for 40 minutes per pound (about 2 hours) or until a meat thermometer registers 185 degrees. Baste frequently during baking with the marinade in the pan.

Allow the roast to stand for 15 minutes before slicing. Serve the marinade as a sauce.

Serves 6.

Rabbit Braised in Coconut Milk
Conejo con Leche de Coco

1 rabbit, 2½ to 3 pounds, cut into serving pieces

1 tablespoon safflower oil

2 tablespoons butter

1 large onion, coarsely chopped

3 to 4 *serrano* chilies, seeded and chopped

6 cloves garlic, finely chopped

1 cup chicken stock

¼ cup lemon juice

1¼ cups coconut milk (page 16)

½ teaspoon crushed dried rosemary or ¼ teaspoon minced fresh

Coconut milk helps to tenderize the meat. It also makes this dish authentically South American and very tasty.

Sauté the rabbit pieces in the oil and butter, turning to brown on all sides. Transfer the rabbit to an ovenproof casserole.

Add more butter and oil to the pan if necessary and sauté the onion, chilies, and garlic until the onion is golden. Add the vegetables to the casserole. Deglaze the pan with ½ cup of the chicken stock and pour into the casserole. Combine the remaining ½ cup of stock, lemon juice, ¾ cup of the coconut milk, and the rosemary and add to the casserole. Cover and bake at 300 degrees until the rabbit is very tender, about 1½ hours.

Remove the rabbit to a hot platter and keep warm. Reduce the contents of the casserole over high heat until the sauce is quite thick. Add the remaining ½ cup of coconut milk, and heat through. Pour the sauce over the rabbit and serve with Coconut Rice (page 156).

Serves 6.

Brazil's National Dish—Black Beans and Meat
Feijoada Completa

Feijoada Completa *is Brazil's great national dish. Restaurants feature it for Saturday lunch, the preferred time to eat it on home turf. It is not a meal for dining* à deux, *but it is perfect for a big, informal gathering. I think it is especially fine on a cold and blustery day but Brazilians eat it with gusto whatever the weather. The recipe that follows would probably feed eight or ten people in Brazil. I think it will adequately serve at least ten or twelve North Americans, and probably more.* Feijoada *is substantial fare and its side dishes are filling, too.*

This recipe calls for all the traditional meats except the pig's tail and four ears. Our butchers do not usually stock these items and I do not believe the dish will suffer from their omission. (However, if you choose to include pig's ears and tail, treat them as follows. Soak four pig's ears and one tail in slightly salted water for two days. Keep refrigerated. Then add the ears and tail to a large pan of fresh water and bring it to a boil. Lower the heat and simmer for ten minutes. Remove the ears and tail and add them to the bean pot after the beans have cooked for one and a half hours.) There should be a selection of both fresh and smoked meats, but substitutions and subtractions are acceptable. Even in Brazil, the cooks make choices. Ingredients also vary in different parts of the country. The smoked tongue is essential and so is the dried beef. The tongue is important to the ritual presentation that varies little from recipe to recipe, from time to time, or from place to place.

Although Feijoada *is first mentioned as late as the nineteenth century and is said to have originated in Rio, most culinary scholars agree that its roots are African. The name, however, comes from the word* feijão, *Portuguese for "bean." Black beans are the most favored, although other varieties are used in some parts of Brazil. Other standard ingredients include a variety of sausages, sun-dried beef called* carne sêca *(for which we may have to substitute beef jerky), fresh pork, cured pork, bacon, smoked tongue, and a pig's foot, tail, and ears. An addition favored by some cooks is a cup or two of orange juice included in the liquid in which the beans are cooked.*

4 cups dried black beans

¾ pound *carne sêca*, in one piece, or an equal quantity of beef jerky

½ pound Canadian-style bacon, in one piece

1 pound corned spareribs

1 smoked beef tongue, about 3 pounds

¾ pound smoked Portuguese sausages (*linguiça*)

1 fresh pig's foot, split

1 pound lean beef, in one piece (chuck or bottom round)

¾ pound fresh, breakfast-type pork sausages

Salt and pepper to taste

2 onions, chopped

3 cloves garlic, minced

2 tomatoes, peeled, seeded, and chopped

1 *hontaka* chili pepper, stem and seeds removed and crushed

2 tablespoons safflower oil

1 tablespoon chopped parsley

Although recipes vary slightly, the serving ritual does not. Feijoada *is an event and the presentation is all-important. The result is a magnificent spread, a groaning board in every sense of the term, and a convivial party feast. The meats are served on a large platter, the beans in a tureen, and the accompaniments, each in a separate dish, are arranged around the two main dishes. Traditionally the diners serve themselves, placing all the food on a single plate. A large plate, one that is not too flat, is obviously best suited to the occasion. A salad of hearts of palm, for which it is acceptable to provide a second plate, is frequently served with the* feijoada.

Many Brazilians drink cachaça *before and during the meal. This is a local, strong, white sugarcane rum that they consume undiluted and consider a digestive as well as a festive libation. In fact, diners who claim to have eaten their fill are urged to drink a little more* cachaça *and to eat another orange slice or two, an act of indulgence guaranteed to make them hungry enough to eat a little more meat and beans. For those who are not connoisseurs of straight* cachaça, *a* Batida paulista *(page 134) is more palatable and is still authentic. It calls for the addition of lemon or lime juice and sugar to the* cachaça. *Although this cocktail is a delightful introduction to the feast, when it comes time to eat, many devotées of* feijoada *prefer a chilled beer as they make their way through the meal.*

It takes time—and organization—and a few large pots—to prepare feijoada completa, *but it is not difficult. Most of the work can be done ahead. There are many steps, but none of them is hard to do.*

The night or day before, wash and pick over the beans. Soak them in cold water to cover for 1 hour. Soak the *carne sêca*, Canadian bacon, and spareribs for 12 hours, each separately.

The next day, put the beans in a pot large enough to hold all the ingredients. A stockpot or "lobster" pot works well. Cover them with fresh water and cook them over low heat for about 1½ hours. Add water as needed to keep the beans covered and stir occasionally so that they do not stick or burn. When the beans are tender, set aside ¼ cup to add to the *Môlho de pimenta e limão* just before serving.

Drain the *carne sêca*. Cover it with cold water and bring it to the boil. Reduce the heat and simmer until the meat is fork-tender, about 1 hour. When cool enough to handle, cut into 1-inch strips and set aside.

Side dishes

Sliced oranges

Môlho de pimenta e limão (page 171)

Fresh onion rings

Arroz blanco (page 157)

Couve à mineira (page 147); spinach or chard may be substituted

Farofa de manteiga (page 174)

Cover the tongue with cold water, bring to the boil, reduce the heat, and simmer for 3 to 4 hours. Add water as necessary to keep the meat covered. When it is tender, remove the tongue from the water and allow it to cool. Then remove the skin, fat, and gristle and set aside.

Drain the Canadian bacon and the spareribs, cover with fresh water, and bring it to the boil. Reduce the heat and simmer, uncovered, for 15 minutes. Drain the meats and set aside.

Place all the meats, *except* the fresh pork sausage, in a large pot and cover with cold water. Bring to the boil, reduce the heat and simmer until the meats are tender, about 1½ hours. Add water as necessary.

Drain all the meats. Add them to the beans. Add the fresh sausage. Simmer until the meats are very tender and the beans are mushy. Season with salt and pepper as desired but be sure to taste first as cured meats add a lot of salt to the pot.

Feijoada may be made up to this point the day before and refrigerated. On the day it is to be served, bring it to room temperature and re-heat it slowly, allowing enough time for the meats to heat all the way through. Stir frequently to prevent sticking.

Sauté the onions, garlic, tomatoes and the crushed chili pepper in the oil until the onions are soft. Remove about 2 cups of beans from the pot and mash them with a potato masher or the back of a spoon. Mix them with the sautéed vegetables and the chopped parsley and then add the combined mixture back to the bean pot. Stir well. Simmer the entire *feijoada* for 30 minutes. Correct the seasoning.

To serve, separate the meats from the beans. Slice each type of meat, so that every guest can taste a piece, however small. On a large platter, arrange the slices of fresh meats on one side, the cured meats on the other, and the tongue down the middle. Ladle a small quantity of the bean liquid over the meats, just enough to moisten them slightly.
The beans, because they are rather soupy, should be served from a tureen or deep casserole dish. Arrange the side dishes separately around the meat platter and the dish of beans.

Serves 10 to 12.

Rum Cocktail
Batida Paulista

1 ounce *cachaça* or other light rum

1 teaspoon egg white

1 tablespoon superfine sugar

½ ounce fresh lemon juice

3 or 4 ice cubes

This is the *drink to serve with* Feijoada. *It is an uncomplicated cocktail that, in Brazil, is made with* cachaça, *the local sugarcane rum. Many cocktails are called* batidas, *a word that may be translated as "whipped" or "beaten."*

Combine the rum, egg white, sugar, and lemon juice in a cocktail shaker and stir to dissolve the sugar. Add the ice cubes, put the top on the shaker, and shake vigorously. Strain into a chilled, old-fashioned glass. Some people like to moisten the rim of the glass and dip it in sugar before adding the cocktail.

Yields 1 drink.

Guinea Pig
Cuy

1 guinea pig per person

Garlic to taste

Salt and pepper to taste

Safflower oil

Guinea pig is an old, popular, and authentic Peruvian dish, especially in the Andes where the little vegetarian rodents are kept in many households. This simple recipe is included as a matter of interest.

Skin and clean the guinea pigs. Soak them in heavily salted water for 3 to 4 hours. Remove from the brine, dry off, and leave uncovered to dry for one hour.

Cut each guinea pig into quarters and rub the pieces with a mixture of garlic crushed with salt and pepper. Fry the pieces in hot oil until they are well browned on all sides. Reduce the heat and continue to cook, turning the pieces frequently to cook well. The meat should be crisp on the outside.

Serve with *Creole Sauce* (page 164).

Vegetables and Potatoes

Verduras y Papas; Legumes e Batatas

South Americans do not eat a great many plainly cooked vegetables. They do, however, use a number of vegetables in their cooking and these include beans of all varieties, corn, and squash. The potato recipes in this section are among the true glories of the South American cuisines. These outstanding dishes are often served as separate courses—and I must concur that it is not too great an honor to bestow upon them.

In the market, Valpariso, Chile

Spicy Avocado
Aguacate Picante

3 or 4 large ripe avocados, peeled and diced

2 cloves garlic

2 onions

2 red or green bell peppers, seeded

2 to 3 *serrano* or *jalapeño* chilies, seeded

2 tomatoes, peeled and seeded

¼ cup olive oil

¼ cup white wine vinegar

Salt to taste

½ pound bacon, diced, fried crisp, and drained well (optional)

South Americans are infinitely imaginative in their use of avocados. Combined with a spicy hot sauce and served as a vegetable, one of our favorite salad ingredients is newly delicious. I like this recipe so much that I keep finding other uses for it. It makes a fine salad when piled on a bed of lettuce or spinach. Add a few flavorful olives and accompany it with hot corn or French bread. As a sauce for plain boiled or baked potatoes, it performs magic.

Peel and dice the avocados and place them in a large colander. Rinse them thoroughly with cold water and drain well. This will prevent their turning dark. Set aside.

Purée the garlic, onions, bell pepper, chilies, and tomatoes in a blender or food processor. Cook the purée in hot olive oil for 2 to 3 minutes. Add the vinegar and salt and simmer over low heat for 20 minutes.

Cool the sauce to room temperature and then *gently* stir in the diced avocado and bacon. The sauce (without the avocados) may be frozen.

Serves 6 to 8 as a side dish.

Bananas with Chilies and Onions
Banana Carioca

6 ripe bananas, cut into 2-inch rounds

⅓ cup safflower oil

1 large onion, finely chopped

4 to 6 *serrano* or *jalapeño* chilies, seeded and finely chopped

Salt to taste

South Americans serve a number of what they call "little dishes" with or before an entrée. This banana dish from Rio de Janeiro is a good example and one that adds extra interest to a pork or chicken dinner. It is quick and easy to prepare. If the bananas are very ripe, the natural sugar they contain will cause them to carmelize, making them especially delicious.

Sauté the bananas in the oil until they are golden brown, turning them frequently and watching them carefully. Remove the bananas from the skillet and set aside.

In the same oil, sauté the onion until it is soft. Mash the bananas and return them to the pan with the onions. Add the chilies and salt to taste. Cook gently for 2 to 3 minutes over low heat stirring constantly. Serve hot.

Serves 6 as a side dish.

Native Caviar—Black Beans

Caraotas Negras

1 cup dried black beans

1 large onion, coarsely chopped

5 tablespoons olive oil

3 cloves garlic, pressed

1 or more *hontaka* chilies, seeds removed and crushed

2 teaspoons cumin seeds, crushed

Salt to taste

This is one version of a black bean dish that is highly regarded by the Venezuelans. They lovingly call it caviar crillo, *"native caviar." It goes well with grilled meats or chicken.*

Cook the beans in lightly salted water until they are tender, about 1 hour. Drain them and set aside.

Sauté the onion in 2 tablespoons of the olive oil until it is soft. Add the garlic, chilies and the cumin and continue to cook for 2 minutes. Add the beans, all or some of the remaining olive oil, and the salt to taste. Mix well.

Serves 6 as a side dish.

Black Beans with Ham Hocks
Frijoles Negros con Jamón

2 cups uncooked black beans

2 ham hocks

2 firm bananas, coarsely chopped (optional)

1 teaspoon paprika

Salt to taste

2 onions, finely chopped

1 tablespoon safflower oil

2 tomatoes, peeled, seeded, and chopped

½ cup chopped cilantro

Black beans, which are popular all over South America, are now widely available in supermarkets and health food stores in the United States. They cook quite quickly, and to keep all the flavor, are best done without long soaking. They have their own distinctive and delicious flavor.

Place the beans in a large pot, cover them with cold water, and bring to the boil. Add the ham hocks, partially cover the pot, and reduce the heat to keep the water just simmering. When the beans are almost tender, about 1 hour, add the bananas, paprika, and the salt, if necessary.

Sauté the onions in the oil until they are soft. Add the tomatoes and cook together for 2 minutes. Add this mixture to the beans and bring just to the boil. Serve, generously garnished with chopped cilantro.

If desired, the ham hocks can be taken from the pot when the beans are finished cooking and the meat removed from the bones. Discard the bones and fat and return the meat to the pot.

Serves 8.

Pickled Black Beans
Frijoles Negros Escabechados

2 cups dried black beans

2 large onions, cut in thick slices

½ cup red wine vinegar

½ pound ham

3 tablespoons safflower oil

½ teaspoon *annatto* powder (optional)

3 cloves garlic, minced

1½ teaspoon cumin seeds, crushed

1½ teaspoon chili powder or 2 *ancho* chilies, seeded and crushed

Salt and pepper to taste

2 hard-boiled eggs

½ cup pitted black olives

Although the name of this somewhat offbeat dish may not be immediately compelling, I urge you to try it because it is delicious. Peruvians serve it with rice but I like it best as a side dish to accompany grilled red meat. It also makes an interesting salad when piled atop a bed of shredded raw spinach and garnished with chopped hard-boiled eggs. It is best served at room temperature whether as a salad or a side dish.

Cook the beans in lightly salted water until they are tender but still hold their shape, about 1 hour. While the beans are cooking, bring the onions to a boil in salted water over high heat. As soon as they boil, drain them completely and combine them in a small bowl with the vinegar. Cut the ham into small pieces.

Heat the oil in a large skillet. Add the *annatto* powder, ham, garlic, cumin, and the chili powder and cook for 2 or 3 minutes. Add the well-drained beans, the onions, and enough of the vinegar to keep the dish moist—it may be necessary to add it all. Stir and cook for several minutes.

Serve garnished with coarsely chopped hard-boiled eggs and black olives.

Serves 6 as a side dish, 4 as a salad.

Cabbage Stew with Chilies and Cilantro
Guisado de Repollo

1 small white cabbage

1 onion, finely chopped

3 tablespoons safflower oil; more if necessary

4 tomatoes, peeled, seeded, and chopped

2 to 4 *serrano* or *jalapeño* chilies, seeded and chopped

Salt and pepper to taste

2 tablespoons chopped cilantro; or more

2 potatoes, peeled, cooked, and coarsely chopped

I am particularly fond of this peasant dish, which is just as good served hot, cold, or at room temperature. Actual amounts, even some ingredients, may be treated casually but it is important not to overcook the cabbage, which should be crisp-tender.

Trim the cabbage. Shred it finely, discarding the core. Blanch it for 5 minutes in lightly salted water. Drain and refresh immediately under cold water. Drain well and set aside.

Sauté the onion in the oil until it is soft. Pour in a little more oil if necessary, add the tomatoes and chilies, and cook to blend well. Add the salt, pepper, cilantro, potatoes, and the cabbage and mix thoroughly. Heat through.

Serves 4 to 6 as a vegetable.

Stuffed Chayote Squash

Chayote Relleno

3 *chayote* squash

2 tablespoons safflower oil

1 onion, finely chopped

¾ pound lean ground round

3 cloves garlic, minced

2 to 3 *jalapeño* chilies, seeded
and minced

3 tomatoes, peeled, seeded, and
chopped

½ teaspoon oregano

½ teaspoon cumin seeds,
crushed

½ cup raisins

½ cup grated Parmesan cheese
(optional)

Chayote, *which is called* xu xu *(pronounced "shoo shoo") in Brazil, is a member of the squash family and is increasingly available in our markets. Among the easiest ways of preparing it is to sauté, in olive oil, peeled and seeded slices of* chayote *that have been dipped in lightly beaten egg and well-seasoned bread crumbs. Cooked until they turn brown on both sides, they may be served hot as a first course or a vegetable side dish. By itself, it is quite bland but lends itself to being combined with other ingredients. The stuffing mixture below is but one of many possibilities.*

Cut the *chayote* in half lengthwise and remove the large, flat seed. Cook the squash in lightly salted water until they are crisp-tender, about 25 minutes, depending on size. Drain them and scoop out most of the flesh leaving a ¼-inch shell. Set the shells aside and chop the flesh.

Heat the oil and sauté the onion until it is soft. Add the meat, garlic, and chilies and continue to cook over medium heat until the meat is no longer pink. Add the tomatoes, oregano, cumin, raisins, and reserved *chayote* flesh. Combine well.

Gently pile the mixture into the reserved shells. Sprinkle with cheese, if desired. Set on a baking dish and bake at 350 degrees for 15 to 20 minutes.

Serves 6.

Seasoned Corn Purée
Humitas

3 cups corn kernels (6 to 8 ears, depending on size)

½ cup milk

2 eggs

½ teaspoon sugar

Salt and pepper to taste

1 to 2 *serrano* or *jalapeño* chilies, seeded and minced

1 onion, finely chopped

2 tablespoons butter; or more if necessary

¾ cup peeled winter squash, finely chopped

2 tablespoons red bell pepper, minced

¾ cup freshly grated Parmesan cheese

Popular throughout South America, but especially in Argentina and Chile, humitas *is an ancient Indian way of preparing corn. Basically it is just puréed corn, with seasonings and cheese and, partly because it is so simple, it challenges the cook to improvise.*

The most succulent versions are made from unripe or very young corn freshly scraped from just-picked ears. Even when prepared from frozen corn kernels, it is an excellent accompaniment for meat or chicken. When the corn purée is wrapped in corn husks and steamed like Mexican tam-ales, it is called Humitas en chala. *The inclusion of winter squash in this recipe is both unusual and delicious.*

Scrape the kernels from the cobs or use frozen, thawed kernels. In a blender or food processor, purée the corn with the milk, eggs, sugar, salt, pepper, and chilies.

Sauté the onion in the butter. When it is soft, add the squash and bell pepper and cook over low heat, stirring frequently for 20 minutes or un-til the squash is cooked. Add the corn mixture and continue to cook un-til it thickens slightly, about 5 minutes. Add the cheese. Remove from the heat and mix well.

Serves 6 as a side dish.

Corn Purée in Corn Husks
Humitas en Chala

For this you must use fresh corn. Husk the corn and place the husks in hot water to cover while preparing the purée.

Scrape the kernels from the corn cobs. Reserve the cobs. They are traditionally used as a cooking rack. Prepare the corn purée according to the recipe on page 144.

When the filling is ready, drain and dry the husks well. Place the corn cobs in a single layer in the bottom of a large pan with a tight-fitting lid. Add water to reach about half way up the cobs.

With the husks as wrappers, make small packages of the filling using about 1 tablespoon for each. Tie them securely with string and place the packages on top of the corn cobs. Cover the pan and simmer gently for about 30 minutes. To serve, remove the packages from the pan. Untie and arrange them on a platter.

Makes about 20 small packages.

Corn and Tomato Pudding
Pudin de Choclo y Tomate

2 cups corn kernels, freshly scraped from the cob, or frozen and thawed

1 cup Münster or Monterey Jack cheese, cut up

4 tablespoons butter, cut up

Salt and pepper to taste

6 eggs

3 tomatoes, peeled, seeded, finely chopped, and *well* drained

3 tablespoons minced cilantro

This pudding, which is similar to a soufflé, has become one of my favorites and I have found that both the cooking methods described below produce good results. The first one produces a dish that holds up well after it is removed from the oven; the second one is lighter and more like a soufflé.

Purée the corn, cheese, and butter in a blender or food processor. Add salt and pepper to taste and then the eggs, one at a time. Process until smooth. By hand, stir in the tomatoes and cilantro and pour the mixture into a buttered 6-cup casserole. Bake at 350 degrees for about 1 hour or until it is set and nicely browned on top.
Serves 4.

For a lighter dish, more like a soufflé, separate the eggs. Follow the recipe above, but add only the yolks of the eggs. Beat the whites until they form soft peaks and gently fold them into the corn mixture after all the other ingredients are combined. Pour into an 8-cup soufflé dish or deep casserole dish and bake at 325 degrees for about 35 to 40 minutes or until the pudding is puffed and golden and set in the center.

Serves 4 to 6.

Kale Greens Mineira-Style
Couve à Mineira

Brazil

2½ pounds kale greens

⅓ cup bacon fat

Kale is a popular vegetable throughout Brazil, a country not otherwise known for its vegetable consumption. It is considered one of the essential accompaniments to Feijoada completa. *For the uninitiated, this recipe is a good introduction to a vegetable we often overlook. Try adding a spoon-ful or two of crisply fried bacon pieces. If kale is not to be found, substi-tute spinach or chard. Double this recipe to serve with* Feijoada *(page 131).*

Wash the kale, trim off the stems, and blanch the leaves in boiling, salted water for 2 minutes. Remove them to a colander and refresh with cold water. Drain well and squeeze by hand to remove as much water as possible. Cut the kale into thin slices.

Heat the bacon fat and toss the shredded greens in it to coat. Sauté them gently until the greens are tender, about 10 minutes. Serve at once.

Serves 6 as a vegetable.

Potato Stew with Chilies and Cheese
Ajiaco de Papas

3 pounds red or white new potatoes

3 cloves garlic, minced

1 onion, finely chopped

2 to 3 *serrano* or *jalapeño* chilies, seeded and finely chopped

2 tablespoons safflower oil

Salt and pepper to taste

Approximately 1 cup evaporated milk or half-and-half

¼ pound *queso fresco* or *feta* cheese, cubed or crumbled

3 hard-boiled eggs, coarsely chopped

This is one of Peru's many really glorious potato dishes. Much of the preparation can be done ahead but be sure to cook the potatoes just before they are to be served and to combine all the ingredients at the last minute.

Peel the potatoes, if desired, and boil them in lightly salted water. When they are done, drain well and cut into cubes.

Sauté the garlic, onion, and chilies in the oil until the onion is golden. Add the milk and potatoes and stir carefully with a wooden spoon, taking care not to mash the potatoes. Add the cheese and eggs and mix just enough to combine.

Serves 6.

Potatoes Arequipa-Style
Papas Arequipeña

½ cup roasted peanuts

½ cup half-and-half

Salt and pepper to taste

2 to 3 *serrano* or *jalapeño* chilies, seeded

½ cup grated Münster cheese

3 green onions, including some tender green

2 pounds small boiling potatoes

6 hard-boiled eggs, cut in half

½ cup ripe olives

Parsley or cilantro

The city of Arequipa in southern Peru has a reputation for very hot food. Potatoes, bland as they are, are receptive to well-seasoned sauces. This dish combines Inca and colonial traditions. Garnished in the typical Peruvian manner with hard-boiled eggs and olives, it is an almost complete super dish. In Peru's aristocratic homes, this like other potato dishes is often presented as a separate course before the entrée.

In a blender or food processor combine the peanuts, half-and-half, salt and pepper, chilies, cheese, and onions. Purée until the mixture is the consistency of a smooth mayonnaise.

Scrub the potatoes and boil them until they are tender. Drain them and cut each one in half. Arrange the potatoes on a heated platter, cut-side down. Pour the sauce over the potatoes. Arrange the hard-boiled eggs and the olives on the platter and garnish with parsley or cilantro.

Serves 6.

Potatoes Bogota-Style
Papas Chorreadas

8 large baking potatoes, peeled and quartered

3 tablespoons butter

1 large onion, finely chopped

3 tomatoes, peeled, seeded, and coarsely chopped

2 to 3 *habañero* chiles, seeded and minced

⅔ cup heavy cream

1¼ cups grated Münster cheese

Salt and pepper to taste

This well-seasoned dish is a specialty of Bogota, Colombia's capital in the highlands. Because it is uncommonly rich, it is an excellent foil for unsauced or grilled red meats, but it is outstanding enough to be served as a separate course, as it frequently is in Colombia.

Boil the potatoes in lightly salted water until they are just tender. Drain and keep warm.

While the potatoes cook, melt the butter and sauté the onion until it is soft. Add the tomatoes and the chilies and continue to cook over medium heat for 5 minutes. Stir in the cream and the cheese and remove the pan from the heat as soon as the cheese *begins* to melt. Spoon the sauce over the hot potatoes and serve at once.

Serves 6.

Potatoes with Cheese
Llapingachos

2 pounds baking potatoes, peeled and cut in half

Salt and pepper to taste

1 large onion, minced

⅓ cup plus 1 tablespoon butter

½ cup cilantro, minced

¼ pound Münster cheese, grated

This is an Ecuadorian dish and it has a number of variations depending on whether it is prepared in the highlands or along the tropical equatorial coast. In their native environment, llapingachos are little patties, but, because the potato-cheese mixture is tricky (and sticky) to fry, I have adapted the recipe for use in a gratin dish. It tastes almost the same, dispenses with some of the oil, and is far easier to prepare and serve.

Sometimes llapingachos *are topped with a fried egg and served with a sliced avocado on the side. On the coast they are often accompanied by fried plantains and a piquant peanut sauce. They can also be served with a simple sauce made by sautéeing peeled, chopped, and seeded tomatoes briefly in butter with a little chopped onion. The recipe for Peanut Sauce is on page 166.*

Boil the potatoes until they are tender. Drain and mash them with the salt and pepper.

Sauté the onion in the 1 tablespoon of butter until it is soft and add it, together with the cilantro, ⅓ cup butter, and cheese to the potatoes and combine well.

Spread the mixture in a lightly buttered gratin dish or shallow casserole and place it under the broiler until little flecks of brown appear on the potatoes. Serve at once with Peanut Sauce or with any of the other accompaniments mentioned above.

Serves 6.

Potatoes Huancayo-Style
Papas a la Huancaina

1 large red onion

Juice of one lemon

Salt and pepper to taste

1 dried *hontaka* chili, seeded and crushed

Lettuce leaves

8 medium baking potatoes, peeled and boiled

2 to 6 *serrano* or *jalapeño* chilies, seeded

1 cup *queso blanco* or Münster cheese

½ cup half-and-half

⅓ cup safflower oil

4 hard-boiled eggs, quartered

16 black olives

In Peru, this dish is accompanied by cooked ears of corn cut into 2-inch lengths. It is best served at room temperature as a first course but it may also be served cold.

Slice the onion thinly and separate the slices into rings. Combine the rings with the lemon juice, salt, pepper, and the *hontaka* chili. Allow this mixture to stand while preparing the rest of the dish.

Line a platter with lettuce leaves. Arrange the cooked potatoes on top.

Purée the fresh chilies, cheese, half-and-half, salt, and pepper in a blender or food processor. Heat the oil in a skillet and cook the purée over low heat until it becomes smooth and slightly thickened. Pour this sauce over the cooked, hot potatoes.

Remove the onion rings from the marinade and strew them on top of the sauce. Garnish the platter with hard-boiled eggs and olives.

Serves 8.

Mashed Potatoes with Meat Filling
Papas Rellenas

Peru

4 pounds baking potatoes, peeled

2 eggs

1 onion, finely chopped

3 cloves garlic, minced

½ pound ground beef

1 tablespoon safflower oil

Salt and pepper to taste

½ teaspoon ground cumin

3 hard-boiled eggs, finely chopped

8 black olives, chopped

2 tablespoons raisins, chopped

All-purpose flour and rice flour combined in equal proportions

Safflower oil for frying

I like to serve this for supper accompanied by a plate of sliced tomatoes and a crisp green salad.

Boil the potatoes in lightly salted water until they are very soft. Drain and, while they are still hot, mash them thoroughly. Add the eggs and mix well.

Sauté the onion, garlic, and meat in the oil until the meat is no longer pink and the onion is soft. Drain off excess fat. Add the salt and pepper, cumin, hard-boiled eggs, olives, and raisins and mix well.

Divide the mashed potato into 6 to 8 portions. Place a portion in the palm of your hand, flatten it, and top it with a spoonful of the meat mixture. Close the potato over the filling to make a sealed package.

Dredge the package lightly in the flour mixture and sauté it in hot oil until it is golden on both sides. Serve at once.

Serves 6 to 8.

Mashed Potatoes with Vegetable Filling

Papas Rellenas con Verduras

2 bunches spinach

1 onion, minced

1 *poblano* chili, seeded and minced

3 cloves garlic, minced

2 tablespoons butter

½ cup parsley, minced

½ cup cilantro, minced

½ teaspoon grated nutmeg

2 hard-boiled eggs, chopped fine

Salt to taste

This filling is an entirely North American variation; a flavorful vegetarian alternative to Mashed Potatoes with Meat Filling (page 154).

Cook the spinach in the water that clings to the leaves when it is washed. When it has just wilted, remove it to a towel, squeeze dry, and chop finely.

Sauté the onion, chili, and garlic in the butter over medium heat until the onion is soft. Combine with the spinach and all the remaining ingredients. Correct the seasoning. Use as a stuffing for mashed potatoes prepared according to the preceding recipe.

Serves 6 to 8.

Potato Roll with Shrimp Filling
Rocambole de Batata

Shrimp Filling (*Recheio de Camarão*)

5 tablespoons butter

1 onion, minced

1 pimiento or red bell pepper, minced

¾ pound fresh shrimp, peeled, cleaned, and chopped

2 tablespoons minced parsley

3 tablespoons flour

1 cup milk

Salt and pepper to taste

Potato Roll (*Rocambole*)

5 baking potatoes, peeled and quartered

2 tablespoons butter, at room temperature

1 cup milk

4 tablespoons freshly grated Parmesan cheese

½ teaspoon minced parsley

1 teaspoon minced cilantro

1 teaspoon baking powder

2 tablespoons flour

3 eggs, separated

Salt and pepper to taste

Cilantro sprigs for garnish

This is a lovely luncheon or light supper dish.

To make the filling, melt 2 tablespoons of the butter and sauté the onion and pimiento until they are soft. Add the shrimp and continue to cook just until the shrimp turns pink. Stir in the minced parsley and set aside.

In a saucepan melt the remaining 3 tablespoons butter and stir in the flour. Using a wire whisk, gradually stir in the milk. Cook over low heat until the sauce is thickened. Stir in the shrimp mixture and correct the seasoning. Cool to room temperature before filling the potato roll.

To prepare the potato roll, boil the potatoes until they are very tender. Drain and mash them. Mix in the butter, ¾ cup of the milk, the cheese, parsley, cilantro, baking powder, and flour. Lightly beat the egg yolks with the remaining ¼ cup milk and add to the potato mixture. Add salt and pepper to taste. Beat the egg whites until they hold soft peaks and fold them into the potatoes.

Line a jelly-roll pan with foil and butter the foil well. Starting in the center, spread the potato mixture on the foil with a rubber spatula. It may not completely fill the pan. Bake at 400 degrees for about 25 minutes or until the top is lightly browned. Remove from the oven and carefully invert onto a damp tea towel. Cool for 5 minutes and then carefully peel off the foil.

To assemble the *rocambole*, carefully spread the cooked potato with shrimp filling, and, using the towel as a helper, roll up, jelly-roll style. Serve warm, cut in 1½-inch thick slices garnished with cilantro sprigs.

Serves 6 to 8.

Rice with Coconut Milk

Arroz con Leche de Coco; Arroz com Leite de Côco

2 cups coconut milk (page 16)

1 cup raisins (optional)

1 onion, finely minced

2 tablespoons safflower oil

2 cups short-grained rice

2 cups chicken stock

Salt to taste

In Brazil, where rice is served at almost every meal, it is frequently cooked with coconut milk for which it has a strong affinity. Along the tropical coasts of Colombia and Venezuela, raisins are often added.

Combine the coconut milk and the raisins and set aside.

Sauté the onion in the oil until it is soft. Add the rice and cook for 2 to 3 minutes. Stir and take care that the rice does not brown. Add the coconut milk, raisins, stock, and salt. Bring to the boil, reduce the heat, cover, and simmer over very low heat until the rice is tender and dry, 20 to 25 minutes.

Remove the pan from the heat and allow to stand, covered, for about 15 minutes or up to 30 minutes. Stir lightly with a fork just before serving.

Serves 6.

White Rice

Arroz Blanco

1 onion, finely chopped

4 tablespoons safflower oil

1 green or red bell pepper,
seeded and cut in quarters

1 clove garlic, minced

2 cups long-grained rice

Salt to taste

4 cups boiling water

This method of preparing rice is popular throughout South America. In Venezuela, it is traditionally served with Pabellón criollo, *but it goes well with almost any meat, poultry, or seafood dish.*

Sauté the onion in the oil until it begins to turn soft. Add the bell pepper, garlic and the rice and stir to coat the rice well. Cook over medium-high heat for 1 or 2 minutes, stirring so that the rice does not brown. Add the salt and the boiling water. Bring the mixture to a boil, cover, reduce the heat, and simmer gently for 20 to 25 minutes or until all the water is absorbed and the rice is tender. Discard the bell pepper.

Serves 4 to 6.

Lentil Stew with Sausage

Chorizo y Lentejas

1 pound *chorizo* (Spanish
sausage)

1 cup *cooked* lentils

1 onion, thinly sliced

1 clove garlic, pressed

1 bell pepper, seeded and
coarsely chopped

2 tomatoes, peeled, seeded, and
coarsely chopped

Salt and pepper to taste

Spanish chorizo *is generally available in several degrees of hotness, so the
piquancy of this hearty and inexpensive dish may be varied depending on
your choice of the sausage. It is best served at room temperature.*

Cut the sausage into bite-sized coins and sauté lightly in a skillet. When
they have rendered most of their fat, remove the sausage and set it
aside.

Drain all but 2 tablespoons of the fat from the skillet and add the lentils, onion, garlic, and bell pepper. Cook slowly, stirring occasionally,
until the lentil mixture turns slightly yellow from the seasonings in the
sausage. Add the tomatoes and the sausage and salt and pepper. Cover
and simmer until the sausage is fully cooked, about 15 minutes. Serve
hot or at room temperature.

Serves 4.

The National Dish of Chile—
A Grand Vegetable Stew
Porotos Granados

1½ cups dried cranberry beans (pea beans are acceptable)

1 large onion, coarsely chopped

4 tablespoons olive oil

1 clove garlic, minced

6 tomatoes, peeled, seeded, and chopped

½ teaspoon basil

1½ teaspoons oregano

½ teaspoon thyme

Salt and pepper to taste

2 cups winter squash (about 1 pound), peeled and cut into ½-inch cubes

⅓ cup corn kernels

Although Chile is a land of sharp geographic contrasts, wherever people live or whatever their station in life, they all eat Porotos granados. *Porotos is the local Indian word for fresh cranberry beans. In Chile's mild climate, these are available fresh year-round.*

This is hearty fare, of Indian origin, and is based on the staple triad of beans, corn, and squash. I have served Porotos granados *a number of times and, always, those who have eaten it have been pleasantly surprised at just how good it is. The* Pebre *sauce to go with it is important and should not be neglected.*

Cover the beans with cold water, bring to the boil, turn off the heat and allow the beans to soak for 1 hour. Change the water, bring the beans to the boil again, reduce the heat, and simmer for 1 hour.

Sauté the onion in the oil until it is soft. Add the garlic, tomatoes, basil, oregano, thyme, salt, and pepper and cook, stirring over medium heat until the mixture forms a thick purée.

When the beans have cooked for 1 hour and are almost tender, add the tomato purée and the squash and continue cooking until the beans are completely done and the squash is mushy. Stir in the corn and cook for an additional 5 minutes. Serve hot with *Pebre* sauce (page 167).

Serves 6.

Sautéed Plantains

Plátanos a Salteados

2 very ripe plantains (see page 24)

1 *jalapeño* chili, seeded and sliced in thin rings (optional)

2 tablespoons butter; more if needed

½ cup sour cream, at room temperature

Although I have not developed a great fondness for them, plantains are important to South American cooking, especially in the tropical and coastal areas. Bananas may be substituted in some recipes but, both the flavor and texture are quite different. Even very ripe plantains are far less sweet than bananas and they are firm enough not to lose their shape and become mushy during even long cooking. The following recipe may be served with plainly prepared pork or chicken.

Peel the plantains and cut into quarters. Cut each quarter in half lengthwise. Sauté the plantains and the chili in butter over medium heat, turning the plantains frequently, until they are nicely browned. Remove to a serving dish and drizzle with sour cream.

Serves 4 as a side dish.

Banana Pancakes
Tortilla de plátano

4 ripe bananas

Juice of 1 lemon

2 tablespoons safflower oil

4 eggs, separated

½ teaspoon vanilla extract

2 cups milk

2 cups flour

2 tablespoons baking powder

½ teaspoon freshly grated nutmeg

½ teaspoon allspice

2 tablespoons sugar

Banana pancakes are excellent for breakfast, brunch or supper. This generous recipe makes enough to feed six hungry people.

Mash the bananas with a fork and sprinkle with lemon juice.

Combine the oil, egg yolks, and vanilla and beat well. Add the milk and beat again.

Combine the flour, baking powder, nutmeg, allspice, and sugar. Add the liquid mixture and stir just to combine. Stir in the bananas. Let the batter stand for 30 minutes.

Beat the egg whites until they form soft peaks. Fold them into the batter. Fry the pancakes on a lightly buttered, hot griddle, turning once. Serve with honey.

Serves 6.

Sauces

Salsas; Môlhos

Well-flavored sauces are common to all the South American cuisines but they are especially important in Bahia where most of the wonderful dishes are time-tested blends of many ingredients. The sauces in which these ingredients are either cooked or served help to pull the exotic combinations together. Outside Bahia, some special sauces have long associations with particular dishes. Others tend toward more general use and many of these, such as Fresh Tomato and Cilantro Sauce and Colombian *Salsa cruda,* are particularly adaptable to our cooking.

This section on South American sauces is not large but it includes the ones essential for particular dishes and in most cases, suggestions for alternate uses.

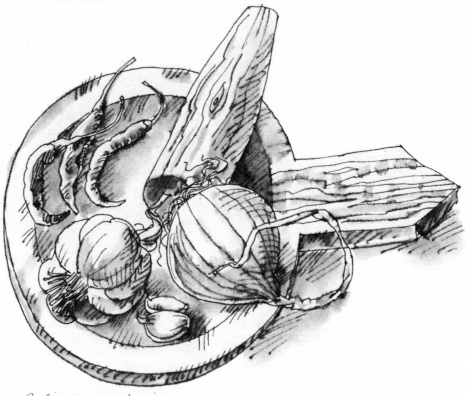

Garlic, peppers and onion

Basic Tomato and Onion Sauce
Salsa de Aliños

2 onions, thinly sliced or finely chopped

2 tablespoons butter

6 tomatoes, peeled, seeded, and chopped

2 cloves garlic, minced

1 cup stock or water

½ cup lemon juice or wine (optional)

Bouquet garni, parsley, cilantro, or any herbs that please

This is the basic sauce with which South American cooks begin countless dishes. It is used to sauté meat, fish, or poultry, to baste roasted or grilled meats, added to the pot with boiled meat, and served as a gravy with the finished dishes. They often make this versatile sauce in large quantities. It keeps in the refrigerator for about a week. Exact proportions vary with the cook but, in general, 3 tomatoes to 1 onion gives good results.

Sauté the onions slowly in butter until tender. Add the remaining ingredients and simmer the sauce, uncovered, until it becomes thick.

Yields approximately 1 cup.

Creole Sauce
Salsa Criolla

2 onions, minced

3 tomatoes, peeled, seeded, and finely chopped

2 *serrano* or *jalapeño* chilies, seeded and minced

2 cloves garlic, minced

1 to 2 tablespoons parsley, minced

Salt and pepper to taste

⅓ cup olive oil

4 tablespoons red wine or red wine vinegar

This sauce is traditionally served with Matambre *(page 122). It is also good with other simple meat dishes.*

Combine the onions, tomatoes, chilies, garlic, parsley, and salt and pepper. Combine the oil and vinegar and add the mixture to the minced vegetables. Mix well and allow to stand for 2 to 3 hours at room temperature.

Yields approximately 2 cups.

Fresh Tomato and Cilantro Sauce
Salsa Cruda Colombiana

4 hot red or green chilies, (such as *habañeros*, *jalapeños*, or *serranos*), seeded

6 green onions

4 tomatoes, peeled and seeded

½ cup cilantro, chopped

Salt to taste

Cruda *simply means "raw" in Spanish. This popular uncooked sauce accompanies many Colombian dishes and is especially good with grilled fish or meat. The proportions are up to the cook so make it as fiery—or as tame—as you choose. It is at its best when freshly prepared with good, ripe tomatoes. It keeps well for up to a week in the refrigerator but if it has been refrigerated, bring it to room temperature before serving on or with hot food.*

Finely chop the chilies, onions, tomatoes, and cilantro. Add salt to taste. Cover and allow to mellow at room temperature for several hours.

Yields approximately 1 cup.

Peanut Sauce
Salsa de Maní

3 tablespoons minced onion

3 tablespoons butter

1 tablespoon minced *jalapeño* chili

1 tomato, peeled, seeded, and coarsely chopped

½ cup ground or finely chopped roasted peanuts

3 to 4 tablespoons water

Salt and pepper to taste

If possible, make this sauce several hours ahead and then reheat it just before serving. It is traditional with Llapingachos *(page 151) but it is good on other potato dishes, too.*

Sauté the onion in the butter for 2 minutes. Add the chili pepper and the tomato and continue cooking until the sauce becomes mushy. Add the peanuts and mix well. Remove from the heat and slowly add the water to make a sauce consistency. Season with salt and pepper to taste.

Yields approximately ¾ cup.

Sauce for Porotos Granados
Pebre

2 tablespoons olive oil

1 tablespoon wine vinegar or lemon juice

½ cup water

½ cup cilantro, finely chopped

1 clove garlic, pressed

½ teaspoon salt

4 to 6 *habañero* chilies, seeded and finely chopped

Traditionally served with Porotos granados *(page 159), Chile's national dish, this simple sauce is also good with grilled meat. The number of hot chiles is variable.*

Combine the oil, vinegar, and water with a wire whisk. Stir in the remaining ingredients and mix well. Correct the seasoning. Allow the sauce to stand at room temperature for about 3 hours. Refrigerated, it will keep for a week.

Yields approximately 2 cups.

Piquant Sauce for Fish
Môlho por Peixe

1 teaspoon cumin seeds

3 cloves garlic

2 teaspoons minced parsley

Salt and pepper to taste

½ cup white wine vinegar

4 tablespoons water

2 tablespoons tomato paste

This sauce is strong and piquant and a fine compliment to otherwise lightly flavored or seasoned food. It need not be limited to fish and I have found it especially good on steamed vegetables.

Pound the cumin seeds, garlic, parsley, and salt and pepper together to make a paste. A mortar and pestle work well for this. Combine the paste with the other ingredients and mix well. Cook over medium heat for 10 to 15 minutes or until the sauce is reduced slightly and the garlic is cooked and loses its raw taste. Pour the sauce over hot fried or broiled fish just before serving.

Yields approximately ¾ cup.

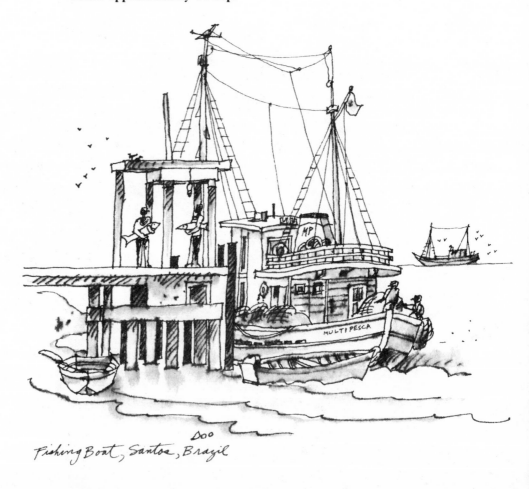

Fishing Boat, Santos, Brazil

Prawn Sauce for Fish
Môlho de Camarãos por peixe

2 tablespoons butter

1 tablespoon flour

1½ cups coconut milk (page 16)

2 green onions, minced

6 medium prawns, peeled, deveined, and finely chopped

¾ cup tomato sauce

Salt and pepper to taste

This pale pink combination of typically Brazilian ingredients creates an elusive flavor and provides a glamorous finishing touch for any broiled or poached fish.

Melt 1 tablespoon of the butter. Stir in the flour and cook for 1 to 2 minutes, taking care that the mixture does not brown. Whisk in the coconut milk and simmer gently for 10 minutes, stirring frequently.

Melt the remaining tablespoon of butter and sauté the onion and the prawns just until the prawns turn pink. Add the tomato sauce and combine this mixture with the coconut milk mixture. Correct the seasoning. Serve warm. If reheating, do not boil.

Yields approximately 2½ cups.

Custard Sauce for Vatapás
Pirão de Arroz

1 cup coconut milk (page 16)

2 cups water

1 tablespoon *dendê* oil, if available

½ cup unsweetened rice flour

Pirão de arroz *is a rather bland and creamy moulded "sauce" for* vatapás. *Its blandness is an asset, making it an appropriate contrast to the multi-flavored* Vatapá de camarão e peixe *(page 92) and* Vatapá de galinha *(page 109). Because the sauce is molded, the presentation is especially attractive.*

Heat the coconut milk, 1½ cups of the water and the *dendê* oil in a saucepan. Combine the rice flour and the remaining ½ cup water and add it gradually to the hot coconut milk mixture. Stir over low heat until it becomes creamy and thick, about 3 to 4 minutes. Turn into a well-oiled 1-quart mold or into 6 individual molds. Refrigerate for 4 to 6 hours.

Yields approximately 3 cups.

Chili and Lemon Sauce
Môlho de Pimenta e Limão

3 to 4 cayenne or *serrano* chilies, seeded

1 clove garlic

1 small onion, quartered

½ teaspoon salt

½ cup lemon juice

This fiery hot Brazilian sauce is traditionally served with vatapás *(pages 92 and 109) and with* Feijoada *(page 131).*

Purée the chilies, garlic, onion, and salt in a blender or food processor. Combine the purée with the lemon juice and allow it to stand for 2 to 3 hours at room temperature. This sauce will keep for several days in the refrigerator but will ferment if kept too long. It freezes well, however.

Yields approximately ¾ cup.

Manioc Meal

Farofa

The manioc (bitter cassava) meal known as farofa *is invariably on Brazilian tables, served either in crockery bowls or in a special shaker called a* farinheira. *The meal is usually simply toasted in a skillet on top of the stove or in the oven.*

Variations of farofa *have become associated with certain dishes. Recipes for three frequently used variations follow. Other ingredients, among them grated raw carrots, chopped hard-boiled eggs, raisins, chopped dried prunes, and grated cheese, may also be added. Since the* farofa *itself is bland and almost tasteless, except to devotées who savor its "subtle, nut-like flavor," it goes with just about anything.*

Toasted Manioc with Dendê Oil
Farofa de Azeite de Dendê

1 cup manioc meal (see page 12)

2 tablespoons *dendê* oil (see page 18)

Turn the manioc meal into a skillet and add the *dendê* oil. Cook and stir until the *dendê* is melted and the mixture is completely blended.

This variation is traditionally served with many of the Bahian specialities including *vatapá*, *xin-xin* and *moqueca*.

Toasted Manioc with Butter

Farofa de Manteiga

1 cup manioc meal (see page 12)

2 tablespoons butter

Substituting butter for the *dendê* oil in the preceding recipe, follow the same procedure. This is the version served with *Feijoada completa*.

Toasted Manioc with Scrambled Egg

Farofa com oro

Half an onion, finely chopped

2 tablespoons butter

1 cup manioc meal (see page 12)

1 egg, lightly beaten

1 teaspoon minced parsley

Salt to taste

Sauté the onion in the butter until soft. Add the manioc and the egg. Stir lightly over low heat until the egg is scrambled and has separated into small pieces. Add the minced parsley and salt to taste. This version is good with roast chicken, steaks, and chops.

Desserts

Postres; Sobremesas

Desserts are not served at the end of a meal in South America as frequently as they are here because very often the last course is fruit. That does not mean that South Americans do not care for sweets. A late-afternoon break for coffee and pastries is common practice everywhere.

Brazilians in particular have a sweet tooth and many of their desserts include too much sugar for my taste. The Brazilians inherited their taste for egg-rich and cloyingly sweet desserts from the Portuguese who developed a taste for these confections during the long Moorish occupation. But they do make a number of truly wonderful cakes, especially those in which nuts, fruits, and spices are combined in a rich mélange.

Avocados are used in a number of delightful South American desserts and, with our constant supply, we can enjoy them here as well.

Fruit and Sweets Stand

Avocado Ice Cream

Gelado do Abacate

3 cups milk

½ cup sugar

½ tablespoon cornstarch

1 tablespoon water

2 eggs

½ cup heavy cream

2 ripe avocados, peeled and pitted

Juice of half a lime

½ teaspoon finely grated lime peel

2 tablespoons powdered sugar

This is delicious. It is rich, delicately flavored, and a lovely pale green color. Serve it with lemon- or orange-flavored cookies or with a spoonful of chopped candied orange peel on top.

Heat the milk and sugar to the boiling point. Add the cornstarch mixed with 1 tablespoon water. Boil the mixture gently for 3 to 4 minutes. Remove from the heat and let cool slightly.

Beat the eggs lightly, pour the warm milk mixture over them, and continue to beat well. Allow this custard to cool and then strain.

Add the cream.

Mash the avocados with the lime juice, lime peel, and powdered sugar until the mixture is smooth. If the avocados are at all fibrous or stringy, press the mixture through a sieve. Combine with the custard.

Freeze, either in the freezer compartment of the refrigerator or in an ice cream freezer.

Yields approximately 1½ quarts.

Avocado Whip
Abacate Batida

Brazil

3 ripe avocados, peeled and pitted

½ cup sifted powdered sugar, or to taste

Juice of 1 lime, or to taste

This light and luscious dessert is always a surprise, especially to those who think avocados belong only in salads and guacamole. *My favorite version is the most simple, but the variations are good, too. Serve all of these with* Amor en pedacos *(page 185) or a plain sugar cookie.*

Combine the avocado, sugar, and lime juice and whip to a smooth consistency with a fork. Serve immediately, piled into dessert dishes.

Serves 4 to 6.

Variation one

3 ripe avocados, peeled and pitted

Juice of 1 lime

½ cup sifted powdered sugar

1 cup milk

¼ cup sweet sherry

Combine all the ingredients and whip to a smooth consistency with a fork. Press through a sieve. Serve chilled.

Serves 4 to 6.

Variation two

3 ripe avocados, peeled and pitted

Juice of 1 lime

2 tablespoons sifted powdered sugar

1 cup (½ pint) vanilla ice cream

Combine the avocados, lime juice, and sugar and whip to a smooth consistency. Add the ice cream and beat with a rotary beater or whisk until it is smooth. Place in the freezer in a shallow dish for about 1 hour but do not allow it to freeze. Stir quickly before serving.

Serves 6.

Almond and Coconut Torte

Torta de Amêndoa e Côco

4 egg whites

1 cup sugar

1½ cups freshly grated coconut, or packaged unsweetened coconut

⅓ cup finely chopped, roasted almonds

1 teaspoon vanilla extract

¾ cup flour, sifted

This dessert is wonderful to serve in the spring with whipped cream and fresh berries.

Beat the egg whites until they are frothy. Gradually add the sugar and continue beating until the meringue is thick and glossy. Fold in the coconut, nuts, and vanilla. Gently fold in the sifted flour.

Line the bottom of a 9-inch springform pan with kitchen parchment or heavy-duty foil. Grease the lining and the sides of the pan well. Pour in the batter and cover it lightly with a circle of foil.

Bake the torte at 350 degrees for 30 minutes. Remove the foil from the top and continue baking for another 30 minutes or until it tests done. Cool in the pan.

Serves 8 to 10.

Banana Cake
Bôlo de Banana

½ cup butter

½ cup sugar

3 large ripe bananas, peeled and mashed

½ teaspoon freshly grated nutmeg

1 teaspoon vanilla extract

1 tablespoon orange or lemon juice

1 egg, well beaten

1½ cups flour

2 teaspoons baking powder

½ cup unsalted cashew nuts, roasted and coarsely chopped

½ cup unsweetened, grated coconut

4 ounces cream cheese, softened

Not overly sweet, this cake can be baked in loaf pans or in layer tins. Put the layers together with softened cream cheese.

Cream the butter and sugar together until they are light. Add the bananas, nutmeg, vanilla, orange juice and the beaten egg. Combine the flour and the baking powder and add to the creamed mixture. Stir in the nuts and the coconut.

Using either one 9- by 5-inch loaf pan or two 9-inch layer cake pans, bake in greased tins at 350 degrees. The loaf will bake in about 1 hour and the layers in about 30 minutes. Cool on a rack.

Serves 10 to 12.

Brazil Nut Cake
Bôlo de Castanha do Pará

6 eggs, separated

1 cup sugar

2 cups finely ground Brazil nuts

1 cup heavy cream, whipped

Brazil nuts are difficult to crack so try to find them already shelled. The best sources are often health food stores. Once the shelled nuts are on hand, this elegant cake is not difficult to make.

Beat the egg yolks and ½ a cup of the sugar together. Beat the egg whites until they are foamy and then gradually add the remaining ½ cup of sugar and continue beating until the mixture is very stiff but not dry. Fold the ground nuts into the egg yolk mixture. Then fold in the egg whites.

Pour the batter into 2 buttered 9-inch layer cake pans and bake at 350 degrees for 35 minutes. Cool the cakes in the pans.

When they are completely cool, put the layers together with half of the whipped cream. Spread the remaining half on the top. Refrigerate the cake unless it is to be served immediately.

Serves 8 to 10.

Cashew Nut Cake

Bôlo de Castanha do Caju

1 cup butter

1 cup sugar

4 eggs, separated

1 cup toasted, unsalted cashew nuts, ground to a meal

Grated rind of 1 orange

2½ cups flour

¾ cup fine dry bread crumbs

3 teaspoons baking powder

1½ cups orange juice

This is a large, firm cake, rather coarse in texture. Unlike so many Brazilian cakes and desserts, it is not cloyingly sweet and makes a nice breakfast or coffee cake.

Cream the butter and sugar together until the mixture is light. Add the egg yolks one at a time and beat well. Add the ground cashews and the orange peel. Combine the flour, bread crumbs, and the baking powder and add to the creamed mixture alternately with 1 cup of the orange juice.

Beat the egg whites until they form soft peaks. Add one-third to the cake batter and stir well. Gently fold in the remaining egg whites. Pour the batter into a buttered Bundt or tube pan and bake at 350 degrees for about 1 hour or until the cake tests done. Cool for 5 minutes in the pan and then turn out onto a deep plate.

Make a number of incisions in the cake with a sharp knife and pour the remaining ½ cup of orange juice slowly over the cake. Cool the cake completely before slicing.

Serves 10 to 12.

Fruit Cake with Wine, Chocolate, and Cloves
Bôlo de Frutas

1 cup raisins

1 cup candied fruit

½ cup Madeira

2 tablespoons soft butter

½ cup finely ground, dry bread crumbs

½ cup finely ground Brazil nuts

1 cup sugar

5 eggs, separated

3 tablespoons unsweetened ground chocolate

½ teaspoon ground cloves

1 tablespoon lemon juice

1½ teaspoon baking powder

Tart jelly, such as red currant

Powdered sugar

This is a rich, moist cake, less dense than our traditional fruit cakes, but, with its unusual combination of wine, chocolate, cloves, and fruit, no less flavorful. Parchment paper, available in kitchen supply stores, is used to line the pans so that the cake layers are easy to remove.

Butter two 9-inch cake pans and line the bottoms with parchment paper. Butter the paper.

Soak the raisins and the candied fruit in the Madeira. Cream the butter, bread crumbs, ground nuts, and the sugar together. Add the egg yolks, one at a time and combine well. Then add the chocolate, cloves, lemon juice, and baking powder and mix well. Add the fruits and wine and again mix well.

Beat the egg whites until they form soft peaks and fold them into the cake batter. Pour the batter into the prepared pans, making sure that the fruit is evenly distributed.

Bake at 350 degrees for about 25 minutes or until the cakes begin to pull away slightly from the sides of the pans and appear quite dry. Loosen the edges and cool in the pans for 10 minutes and then turn the cakes out onto racks to cool completely. Put the layers together with jelly and dust the top with powdered sugar.

Serves 10 to 12.

Egg Sweets
Huevos Quimbos

6 egg yolks

1 cup water

1 cup sugar

2 tablespoons rum (optional)

These surprisingly tasty and very unusual little cookies are, for an unknown reason, named after the Quimbaya, an extinct tribe of Colombian Indians. The cookies puff up in the oven but subside as they cool.

Beat the egg yolks until they are stiff and spread them evenly onto a shallow, buttered, 8-inch-square baking dish. Bake at 350 degrees for 30 minutes. Cool. With small, shaped cutters or a sharp pointed knife, cut the custard into fancy shapes or, simply into small squares.

Combine the sugar and water in a saucepan and cook it over medium heat until it forms a thin syrup. When it is cool, add the rum and pour the syrup over the cookies. Remove them from the syrup after about 1 hour and place them on a rack to dry. Refrigerate if not serving immediately.

Yields about 3 dozen cookies, depending on the size.

Love in Fragments

Amor en Pedacos

Brazil

½ cup sugar

¼ cup butter

5 whole eggs

8 tablespoons unsweetened rice flour

2 egg whites

2 tablespoons sugar

½ cup chopped, toasted cashew nuts

This is an example of the playful and imaginative names Brazilians have bestowed upon many of their sweet treats. Most of the names, as well as the recipes, date from the days of the Big Houses of the sugar plantations. The cookie part of this confection is very eggy and has a soft, but solid texture.

Cream the sugar and the butter together. Beat in 1 egg and 2 tablespoons of the rice flour. Repeat this process 3 more times until all the rice flour has been incorporated. Then add the last egg and beat thoroughly.

Spread the batter evenly in a buttered 8-inch-square pan and bake at 350 degrees until the cookie is firm, 10 to 15 minutes.

Beat the egg whites until they are frothy. Gradually add 2 tablespoons sugar while continuing to beat, until the meringue is thick and glossy. Spread it on the cookie and sprinkle with chopped cashews.

Return to the oven until the top is lightly browned. Cut into small pieces.

Yields about 3 dozen, depending on size of the pieces.

Cheese Custard
Flan de Queso

1½ cups cottage cheese

1 can (14 ounces) condensed milk

1½ cups water

4 eggs

This is a pleasant, light dessert to serve with fresh or stewed fruit. Typical of many South American recipes, it relies on canned condensed milk to replace both the milk and sugar. Cottage cheese balances the sweetness.

Drain the cottage cheese in a colander for 15 minutes and discard any liquid. Place the drained cottage cheese, condensed milk, and water in a blender or food processor and mix it until it is very smooth. Add the eggs and process just long enough to incorporate them thoroughly. Pour the mixture into a shallow 1-quart baking dish and bake at 325 degrees until it is set, about 30 to 40 minutes. Serve at room temperature or chilled.

Serves 6.

Fresh Fruit Pudding
Pudin de Fruta

Colombia

4 ripe mangos, peeled and thinly sliced

¾ cup sugar

½ cup water

1 teaspoon cornstarch, dissolved in 1 tablespoon water

2 eggs, separated

½ teaspoon ground cinnamon

2 tablespoons butter

Mangos are perfect for this light pudding but other fruit are good, too. I have tried it using 2 papayas and the strained pulp of 4 passion fruit, a combination that always reminds me of the tropics.

Combine the mangos, sugar, and water in a saucepan and cook over medium heat for 15 minutes. Stir frequently. Beat the egg yolks, add the cornstarch and water, and add this mixture to the mango mixture. Continue to cook and stir for 2 to 3 minutes or until the custard is thick and smooth.

Remove from the heat and stir in the cinnamon and butter. Allow the custard to cool slightly.

Beat the egg whites until they form soft peaks. Fold them into the custard and pile it into dessert dishes. Chill before serving.

Serves 6.

Plantain Dessert

Plátanos Caramel; Banana caramelo

2 very ripe plantains (see page 23), peeled and cut into ½-inch coins

4 tablespoons butter

4 tablespoons brown sugar

Freshly grated nutmeg

One of the simplest of desserts. Bananas may be substituted.

Melt the butter and sugar in a heavy skillet. Add the plantain and sauté over medium heat until they are cooked and carmelized, about 10 to 15 minutes. Stir frequently. Dust with nutmeg and serve warm.

Serves 4 to 6.

Pumpkin Pudding
Pudim de Abóbora

Brazil

1 cup half-and-half

3 eggs, lightly beaten

⅔ cup brown sugar, packed

1 cup cooked, puréed pumpkin, or winter squash

2 tablespoons lemon juice

½ teaspoon grated lemon peel

½ teaspoon ground cinnamon

¼ teaspoon ground cloves

½ teaspoon allspice

This is a rather dense pudding, similar to our pumpkin pie filling. You may substitute winter squash.

Combine all the ingredients and mix well. Pour the batter into a buttered, 1-quart ovenproof casserole or soufflé dish set in a pan of hot water. Bake at 350 degrees for about 1½ hours or until a knife inserted in the center comes out clean. It may take less time, depending on the shape of the container. Cool to room temperature and serve with whipped cream or pouring cream.

Serves 6 to 8.

Sweet Milk Pudding

Dulce de Leche; Doce de Leite

6 cups milk

1 pound sugar

1 piece vanilla bean, about
1 inch long

This dessert is popular throughout South America where it is also called Natillas piuranas *and* Manjar blanco. *It is really nothing more than milk and sugar simmered and stirred together until the mixture becomes caramelized and slightly thick. It is then eaten as it is, with fruit, or as a sauce for other desserts. This confection should be served in small portions and, ideally, with a cup of strong black coffee.*

Because it is time consuming and requires constant attention, busy South American cooks sometimes cheat a little. They remove the label from an unopened can of sweetened condensed milk and simmer the can in a saucepan of water until the contents are caramelized. A word of caution: This method of cooking the contents of an unopened can is not entirely safe. I do not recommend it because the can might explode. The recipe for the original, perfectly safe, method follows.

Combine all the ingredients and cook over medium-high heat, stirring occasionally until it begins to thicken. Reduce heat to low and stir and cook for about 1½ hours or until a spoonful dropped in a cup of cold water forms a soft ball. Remove the milk from the heat and stir constantly and vigorously while it cools. Refrigerate.

Serves 6 to 8, depending on how it is served.

Seasonal Menus

To show how the recipes in this book can work together, I have created sixteen complete menus that range from informal seasonal luncheons to an authentic Brazilian feast for a crowd and a South American-inspired Thanksgiving dinner. Each menu includes dishes that, I believe, complement one another but the choices are by no means definitive. Other, equally satisfying combinations await adventurous and creative cooks. And, of course, no menu need be restricted exclusively to South American foods. A well-chosen dish from Colombia or Peru or Paraguay, or from any South American country, can add excitement to the old and familiar; the tried and true.

These suggested menus follow the North American conventions of ordering a meal. The following menu for a modern Peruvian luncheon illustrates a remarkable difference in customs. For the first course, a *piquero* or large selection of dishes usually served as entrées but cooked as appetizers are set out on a table. Guests circulate around the table and fill their plates from the choices of: potatoes in *Huancayo* sauce, *causa* (mashed, seasoned potatoes), *ocopa* (potatoes in sauce), *escabeche* (pickled chicken or duck), *chicharrones* (fried pork), *anticuchos* (marinated beef-heart kebobs), black pudding, fried *yuca*, fried sweet potatoes, boiled potatoes and boiled corn. All this is accompanied by *pisco* sours. The main course might be one of these: chicken with rice, chicken chili or pickled pork with beans. For dessert, a purple corn jelly and *chicha de jora*, a strong alcoholic drink made from fermented corn, would be served. Such a meal is not typical north of the Rio Grande. Nor is the presentation. Even though they are all delicious, the number of substantial dishes that comprise this meal is far larger than we would choose to eat at one sitting. Fortunately, we can plan our South American meals differently.

Buen apetito and *buen provecho*.

A Spring Luncheon

Although fish *anticuchos* must be broiled just before serving, they are quickly done, and the other parts of this simple spring luncheon may be prepared well ahead. The avocados, as their name indicates, and the basting sauce for the fish are spicy, the Cariocan salad a cool counter-part. Decorate the unfrosted banana cake with spring flowers for a festive finale.

Spicy Avocados (Aguacate picante) *(page 137)*
Marinated Fish on Skewers (Anticuchos de pescado) *(page 52)*
Grapefruit-Cucumber Salad (Salada carioca) *(page 55)*
Banana Cake (Bôlo de banana) *(page 180)*
Coffee or Tea

A Summer Luncheon

Unless it is an exceptionally hot day, too hot for soup, generous bowls of Green Corn Soup are a fine way to appreciate the delicate flavor of really fresh, young corn. No need to serve it piping hot. Let people guess what gives the ice cream its beautiful pale green color and elusive flavor. Although most will probably guess incorrectly, they may promptly accept a second helping.

Pickled Fish (Ceviche) *(page 53)*
Green Corn Soup (Locro de choclo) *(page 86)*
Cheese Biscuits (Biscoitos de queijo) *(page 58)*
Avocado Ice Cream (Gelado do abacate) *(page 177)*
Iced tea or Coffee

Fall Luncheon #1

The aroma of freshly baking (or reheating) *empanadas* creates a warm welcome and provides a hint of good things to follow. The delicate Apple Soup, served in small cups at room temperature, is a pleasant accompaniment to the savory Corn and Tomato Pudding. Whipped avocados take but a few minutes to prepare when all the ingredients, including the peeled avocados, are ready and waiting (see note on peeling avocados ahead of time on page 11).

Savory Turnovers (Empanadas) *(pages 59–67)*
Apple Soup (Sopa de manzanas) *(page 70)*
Corn and Tomato Pudding (Pudin de choclo y tomate) *(page 146)*
Avocado Whip (Abacate batida) *(page 178)*
Coffee or Tea

Fall Luncheon #2

This simple fall luncheon is both hearty and easily transportable. It is wonderful eaten outside if the weather cooperates. Although pickled black beans are not served this way, as a salad, in their native Peru, when piled on a bed of shredded raw spinach and garnished with olives and quartered hard-boiled eggs, they are an elegantly informal entrée salad. For the compote: Simmer mixed dried fruit and sugar and lemon peel to taste in water to cover for fifteen minutes. Cool to room temperature. Add fresh seedless grapes and serve with South American nuts—cashews, peanuts, and Brazil nuts—on the side.

Pickled Black Bean Salad (Frijoles negros escabechados) (page 141)
Fresh and Dried Fruit Compote
Cashews, Peanuts, and Brazil nuts
Coffee and Tea

Winter Luncheon #1

This menu is particularly fine when the weather is not. *Ajiaco bogatano* is an exceptionally well-seasoned chicken and potato soup and *Sopa paraguaya*, despite its name, is a rich, onion and cheese cornbread. Although one is from Colombia and one from Paraguay, they are an admirable combination.

*Chicken and Potato Soup (*Ajiaco bogatano*) (page 79)*
*Corn Bread (*Sopa paraguaya*) (page 84)*
*Egg Sweets (*Huevos quimbos*) (page 184)*
Coffee or Tea

Winter Luncheon #2

The fine Potato Roll makes an elegant luncheon dish and requires little more than a crisp salad to complete the meal. Any number of edible garnishes are appropriate, including additional shrimp, hard-boiled eggs, olives, tomatoes, cilantro, parsley, or watercress.

*Potato Roll (*Rocambole de batata*) (page 155)*
*Tossed Green Salad with Hearts of Palm (*Ensalada verde mixta con palmitos*)*
*Avocado Whip (*Abacate batida*) (page 178)*
Coffee or Tea

A Spring Dinner

Vatapá is one of the great dishes of Bahia and the rest of this spring dinner menu is decidedly Brazilian as well. Properly exotic, it is not difficult to prepare and much of the work can be done ahead. Nasturtiums, natives of Peru, add a beautiful, colorful, and edible garnish to the pale coconut soup.

Spicy Avocados (Aguacate picante) (page 137)
Creamy Coconut Milk Soup (Sopa de leite de côco) (page 74)
Chicken in Peanut Sauce (Vatapá de galinha) (page 109)
Rice with Coconut Milk (Arroz com leite de côco) (page 156)
Sliced Oranges
Banana Cake (Bôlo de banana) (page 180)
Coffee or Tea

avocados in Peruvian pot, with pineapple

A Summer Dinner

Every item on this menu is perfect for a warm summer evening. The soup is smooth and cool, the Chicken Chili as hot as the cook chooses to make it. Strips of roasted, sweet red, yellow, and green peppers and a generous amount of chopped cilantro turn an ordinary tossed green salad into a South American star.

Pickled Fish (Ceviche) *(page 53)*
Hearts of Palm and Coconut Milk Soup (Sopa de palmito e de leite de côco) *(page 75)*
Chicken Chili (Ají de gallina) *(page 104)*
Corn on the Cob
Tossed Green Salad
Avocado Ice Cream (Gelado do abacate) *(page 177)*
Coffee or Tea

A Fall Dinner

The Banana and Bean Dip is filling so keep the portions small to save room for the Beef Pie with fruit, which is a special dish, delicious, different, and quietly spectacular. Please don't be put off by the preparation time—it is worth it and not as long as it appears. This is wonderful party fare. Make the Cheese Custard the day before and refrigerate, but bring it to room temperature for serving.

Banana and Bean Dip with Tortilla Chips (Entremés de banana y frijoles) *(page 49)*
Peanut Soup (Sopa de maní) *(page 76)*
Beef Pie with Apricots (Pastel de carne y albaricoque) *(page 118)*
Tossed Green Salad
Cheese Custard (Flan de queso) *(page 186)*
Coffee or Tea

A Winter Dinner

Anticuchos are authentic, surprisingly good and not infrequently appreciated even by those who do not, at first, know what they are eating. The satin-smooth Chickpea Soup is a perfect complement to the savory Pork with Lemon. Pineapple, mango, papaya, and banana will help create a fruit salad with a South American flavor.

*Marinated Beef Hearts (*Anticuchos*) (page 50)*
*Chickpea Soup (*Sopa de garbanzos*) (page 72)*
*Pork with Lemon (*Cerdo con limon*) (page 128)*
*White Rice (*Arroz blanco*) (page 157)*
*Fruit Salad (*Ensalada de fruta*)*
*Almond and Coconut Torte (*Torta de amêndoa y côco*) (page 179)*
Coffee or Tea

A Spring Buffet Party

This party buffet menu features entrées of chicken, lamb, and shrimp and is planned to please many tastes and a large group. Cheese Custard and Fresh Fruit Pudding, which complement each other as desserts, are best served at room temperature. Peaches, nectarines, apricots, and mangos (or a combination) are good choices for the fruit pudding.

*Grapefruit and Cucumber Salad (*Salada carioca*) (page 55)*
*Couscous with Chicken (*Cuscuz de galinha*) (page 111)*
*Lamb Casserole (*Cazuela de cordero*) (page 125)*
*Bahian Shrimp Stew (*Moqueca de camarão*) (page 95)*
*White Rice (*Arroz blanco*) (page 157)*
*Tossed Green Salad with Avocados (*Ensalada verde con aguacate*)*
*Cheese Custard (*Flan de queso*) (page 186)*
*Fresh Fruit Pudding (*Pudin de fruta*) (page 187)*
Coffee or Tea

A Fall Buffet Party

These are spicy dishes well suited to an informal fall buffet party. Prepare the *anticuchos* on six- to 8-inch wooden skewers as individual servings. The Stuffed Flank Steak is impressive and the Fish in Tangerine Sauce both different and surprisingly delicious. Keep the green salad simple so as not to compete with the various flavors of the entrées.

*Marinated Beef Hearts (*Anticuchos*) (page 50)*
*Cabbage Stew (*Guisado de repollo*) (page 142)*
*Potatoes Arequipa-style (*Papas arequipeña*) (page 149)*
*Stuffed Flank Steak (*Matambre*) (page 122)*
*Fish in Tangerine Sauce (*Peixe com môlho de tangerina*) (page 99)*
Tossed Green Salad
*Cashew Nut Cake (*Bôlo de castanha do pará*) (page 182)*
*Almond and Coconut Torte (*Torta de amêndoa y côco*) (page 179)*
Coffee or Tea

A Winter Buffet Party

Empanadas are perfect offerings with drinks before dinner and are equally good when included as part of the buffet spread. All the dishes for this party menu can be as spicy as the cook chooses to make them.

*A Variety of Savory Turnovers (*Empanadas*) (pages 59–67)*
*A Grand Vegetable Stew (*Porotos granados*) (page 167)*
*Potatoes Bogota-style (*Papas chorreadas*) (page 150)*
*Beef Montevideo-style (*Biftek a la montevideo*) (page 117)*
*Stuffed Stripe Bass (*Corvina rellena*) (page 91)*
Tossed Green Salad
*Brazil nut Cake (*Bôlo de castanha do pará*) (page 181)*
*Peruvian Sweet, Love in Fragments (*Amor en pedacos*) (page 185)*
Coffee or Tea

Feijoada Completa, the National Dish of Brazil

An internationally acclaimed feast, this menu requires more than the usual amount of time to prepare, but none of the tasks is difficult. Do not make *Feijoada completa* for fewer than ten or twelve hungry people unless you want a good deal left over. A *feijoada* party should be informal and the food the featured event.

Black Beans and Meat, both fresh and cured (page 131)
Sautéed Kale (Couve à mineira) *(page 147)*
Sliced Oranges
*White Rice (*Arroz blanco*) (page 157)*
*Manioc Meal (*Farofa de manteiga*) (page 174)*
Onion Rings
*Rum Cocktail (*Batida paulista*) (page 134)*
Beer
Fresh Fruit
Coffee

A Summer Picnic

Many South American dishes are perfect for picnics. *Empanadas*, of course; and Spicy Avocados, for which the sauce should be prepared at home and combined at the site. They are delicious rolled in lettuce leaves or piled into pieces of *pita* bread. Stuffed Chayote and *Causa* should be served at room temperature, but keep the Pickled Chicken cool so that the gelatin remains firm. Egg Sweets and fresh fruit are a fine dessert and good for nibbling later as well.

*Savory Turnovers (*Empanadas*) (pages 59–67)*
*Spicy Avocado (*Aguacate picante*) (page 137)*
Stuffed Chayote (Chayote relleno) *(page 143)*
*Pickled Chicken (*Escabeche de pollo*) (page 107)*
*Mashed Potato Salad (*Causa*) (page 56)*
*Egg Sweets (*Huevos quimbos*) (page 184)*
Fresh Fruit
Coffee or Tea

A South-American-Inspired Thanksgiving Dinner

Probably no American meal is more a set piece than The Thanksgiving Dinner. One slight change in the menu can cause worries and complaints out of all proportion. For the adventurous cook who would risk a complete change, however, this menu provides a delicious and festive alternative. The traditional turkey, pumpkin, and mashed potatoes are all included. Fruit paste in a great variety of flavors is sold in Latin markets and is generally served with fresh white cheese. Cream cheese is a good substitute.

Banana and Bean Dip (Entremés de banana y frijoles) *(page 49)*
Pumpkin Soup (Locro de zapallo I) *(page 88)*
or
Apple Soup (Sopa de manzanas) *(page 70)*
Puréed Seasoned Corn (Humitas) *(page 144)*
or
Pumpkin Stew (Locro de zapallo II) *(page 89)*
Banana, Chile, and Onion (Banana carioca) *(page 138)*
Turkey Casserole (Cazuela de pavo) *(page 114)*
or
Chicken in Fruit Sauce (Galinha com môlho de frutas) *(page 106)*
Sautéed Kale (Couve à mineira) *(page 147)*
Mashed Potatoes with Cheese (Llapingachos) *(page 151)*
Fruit Cake (Bôlo de frutas) *(page 183)*
Quince Paste with Cheese (Dulce de membillo y queso)

Part III

Origins and Influences

Indian Influences
on the Food

The Indian influence on modern South American cuisines is often elusive and, for a number of reasons, limited. Even before the Conquest, the Indian population was never very large. Most of the original inhabitants lived in small, isolated groups and had not progressed much beyond the primitive state. Soon after the Europeans arrived, most of the Indians disappeared almost completely. The Spaniards did not treat them gently and diseases, until then unknown to them, took a heavy toll. The natives left little behind because they had little to leave.

The exception to this sad story was the great Inca Empire that the conquerors found flourishing in the Andean highlands of what is now Peru, Bolivia, and Ecuador and the northern parts of Chile and Argentina. Scholars now believe that this civilization had probably reached its height and quite possibly its full potential, when Pizarro arrived in 1531. Other notable cultures on the southern continent preceded the Incas, most of them also in Peru, but they had disappeared even before the Incas emerged.

Although a search for Indian influences on South American cuisines begins and all but ends in the highlands, the great Inca Empire itself contributed little. Beyond being a necessity, food was not important to them and, from what we know, meals with the Inca compared poorly with the lavish spreads prepared by Montezuma for Cortes and his captains. We have no record of Pizarro receiving, or requesting, an invitation to dinner. The Incas' interests lay elsewhere. Builders, engineers, and administrators, they constructed awe-inspiring bridges and an exceptional road system throughout their vast empire. They terraced their poor agricultural land to grow the crops they needed. Although we have no reports of lavish banquets or bountiful food markets, the fault may lie with the chroniclers.

Corn, which preceded potatoes in the Andean highlands, was fundamentally important to the rise of more advanced societies in those regions. Potatoes, however, were better suited to the difficult terrain, the colder climate, and the high altitudes and, by the time the Inca Empire reached its zenith, they were the staple food crop. Corn gave way to potatoes at the highest altitudes, but it is adaptable to a wide range of conditions and continues to play an important role in the diets of rich and poor throughout much of South America. *Sara Mamma*, the ancient corn mother, is still venerated at annual ceremonies in parts of the Andes today and a stroll through a large produce market in any sizable South American city is an eye-opening experience. Corn on its native continent comes in a staggering variety of shapes, and sizes, and colors. Ears range from the short and stubby, almost round, to huge things well over a foot long with kernels twice the size of hominy. From basic yellow, to white, red, purple, and black, it is a colorful and fascinating sight. The giant white corn that was grown by the Incas is still grown today.

In Colombia, both in the highlands and on the coasts, the cornmeal cakes called *arepas* are the daily food of the poor. In many parts of the Andes, particularly in Bolivia and Peru, a brew called *chicha* is made from fermented corn and, in a probably unintended display of ecumenicalism, twentieth century Indians still honor their age-old god *Pacha Camac* with pitchers of *chicha* at the same time that they celebrate the Roman Catholic festival of Corpus Christi. In Patagonia, the sparsely populated and windswept region of southern Chile, the Araucanian Indians welcome visitors with a home-brewed corn liquor called *muday*. It is fortified with saliva and may be argument enough against too much integration of cuisine.

Wheat was imported soon after the Conquest and supplemented the diets of the Europeans and later generations of creoles, especially in the large cities. However, corn never lost its pre-eminence. For the Indians throughout the continent, wheat has had little effect on their cooking and eating habits.

Important as corn is elsewhere on the continent, potatoes remain the daily food of the highland Indians. The old agricultural terraces, buttressed by stone walls and constructed originally to grow corn, are still in use. Today they support potato patches—along with some corn, beans, and rice. Fresh potato soup, its flavor accented by the addition of a few hot chili peppers, is likely to be standard fare for many families today. Cheese and herbs are added when available and affordable.

As soon as the first cows arrived from Europe, the Spaniards taught the Indians to make cheese, but whether it was the Spanish or the Indians who first thought of the combination of cheese and potato is not known. It was, however, an outstanding idea, one that has given us some of South America's most distinguished culinary creations. The little potato patties called *Llapingachos* (page 151) are a wonderfully rich and popular Ecuadorian dish that could not have been made before the arrival of butter, cheese, and onions. The same is true of *Causa* (page 56), a unique Peruvian dish of mashed potatoes, and there are many others.

There must be as many varieties of potatoes as there are of chile peppers and corn. Markets display huge mounds of potatoes, small piles of potatoes, large, lumpy sacks of potatoes, and still more potatoes. Well over one hundred varieties are known. Some are as tiny as pebbles, some are black, others are yellow, blue, or pink.

The rituals and ceremonies that develop around essential foods in primitive societies are often naively resistant to change. To ensure a successful crop, the Aymara Indians in Bolivia still perform an ancient rite when planting potatoes. Heralded by flute players, cups of the corn brew, *chicha*, are poured onto the ground as an offering to *Pacha Mamma*, the Earth Mother. *Chicha* is also ceremoniously offered to several specially chosen potatoes that are then sliced and stuffed with coca leaves. The impregnated potatoes are planted first. Then everyone gathers around, drinks some *chicha*, and the real planting begins. In some areas, the ritual also includes a llama sacrificed as an offering to *Pacha Mamma*.

The little guinea pig (*cuy*) has been around even longer than the potato and before the Spanish arrived it was just about the only source of animal protein in the Indian diet because llamas were seldom killed for food. The small vegetarian rodents have been known since Peru's Initial Period, *circa* 1750–900 B.C. Still abundant, they are eaten in the highlands by all who can afford them.

In landlocked Paraguay, where ninety percent of the population is of mixed Spanish and Guarani Indian blood, the modern cooking reflects this heritage. The weather fluctuates throughout the year and thick, potato-rich stews, similar to Spanish *cocidos*, are popular when it is cold. This small country is also the home of *yerba maté*, the caffeine-laced herb tea consumed throughout the continent. In Paraguay, Argentina, and Uruguay, where it is most popular, it is drunk at all hours.

Yuca and *manioc*, the two other starchy staples in the pre-Conquest diet, still provide sustenance for large numbers of South Americans. *Yuca*, the nontoxic sweet cassava (see page 12), is easily grown and inexpensive. It is prepared in many of the same ways as potatoes but, because it is almost tasteless, it remains far less interesting and has the added failing of offering no nutritional value. Bitter cassava or manioc (see page 13) is the all-important legacy from the Indians of the Amazon jungle. They were using it as a food when the Portuguese arrived in what is now Brazil.

Communications and travel have never been easy in South America. In remote areas and even in some not so remote, they are still difficult. In the highlands, where little has really changed since Inca times, just managing to exist is not easy. On many nights the temperature drops below freezing and to combat the altitude-induced lethargy everyone chews coca leaves. In the socialistic Inca society all members were provided with food. Today there is not enough. Still, in recent years, populations have increased significantly in the Andes, so that the actual number of people eating what may be called Indian food is greater today than it was in Inca times. In general, the Indians were in no hurry to adopt the ways or the foods of their conquerors and, in isolated areas, they have adopted little to this day.

When Francisco Pizarro marched into Cuzco with his small band of men and horses, he conquered the Incas without great difficulty. He was tricky and deceitful but the Incas were torn by civil war and frightened by the horses, which they had never seen before. The Portuguese, too, easily conquered the natives and took over almost completely. Since then, the upper classes everywhere in South America have consistently rejected most of their Indian heritage—including much of the food.

The African Influence

Salvador, better known as Bahia, is an African city on the northern coast of Brazil. Today its old section seems past its prime but the people smile and the atmosphere is relaxed and cheerful. Plentiful food, encountered almost immediately from innumerable street vendors, is ingeniously flavored and prepared and offered with love and respect.

Among the South American cuisines, the food of this city stands alone. It owes its inspiration to the West African slaves imported by the Portuguese to work the sugarcane plantations in the late fifteen hundreds. The newcomers began almost immediately to modify both the native Indian and the Portuguese dishes and to combine them with their own traditional and highly original cooking methods and ingredients. Soon the African women had taken over the kitchens of the plantation Big Houses and, over the years, their eclectic mingling of ingredients and cooking methods has given Brazil's Bahian region a truly distinctive cuisine, recognized and appreciated today all over the world.

When the first Portuguese colonists arrived in what is now Brazil, they found a small and primitive Indian population whose lives neither rivaled nor resembled the rich and highly organized civilization of the Incas. Much of the land, however, was fertile and, of necessity, agriculture became the economic basis for the Portuguese colonial society. Sugarcane was imported from the Madeira Islands and slaves from West Africa to care for it. The patriarchal Big Houses were established and with them a life-style that has affected Brazilian food, especially in Bahia, to this day.

Although still considered a developing country, Brazil, as one look at the skylines of most of its major cities makes dramatically clear, has enjoyed a good deal of development already. The futuristic capital of Brasilia, the endless highrises lining Rio's glamourous beaches, the sprawling megalopolis that São Paulo has become, and the miles of cranes and big ship docks that make Santos the busiest port on the continent, all speak for themselves. Salvador, too, has grown—and outgrown—its original clifftop situation overlooking a beautiful bay. More than any of the better known Brazilian cities, it retains its considerable colonial charm. With 165 grandly baroque, gilded, and highly decorated churches and a wealth of lovely old homes and public buildings, it boasts some of the finest colonial architecture on the continent.

Lively and lovely it is, and tinged with an elusive sense of mystery that adds yet another dimension. Whether *Candomblé*, the still-practiced voodoo cult, directly affects the food of Bahia is not established, but it is certain that the conversion of the Africans to Christianity remains a task uncompleted. The two religions manage, even in sophisticated Rio, to exist side by side.

The African influence on the foods of Brazil spreads out from Bahia and gradually diminishes in the hinterlands of the huge country. A number of the foods essential to the cuisine as it has evolved were brought to the New World by the slaves who found both the climate and geography of their new homes almost the same as those they had left behind. Foods indigenous to Latin America, such as chili peppers and beans, the Africans adopted enthusiastically.

It is often the interesting variety of ingredients that creates the unique Bahian dishes. One of these ingredients, the ubiquitous *dênde* oil, is a crude cooking oil extracted from the datelike nut of the African and South American palm. Another is the *malagueta* pepper, which can only be called exceptionally hot and, it would seem, made to order for the Bahian taste. *Malaguetas* are natives of the New World but, when introduced to Africa many years ago, they became an important cooking ingredient there and then returned to South America with the slaves.

The Portuguese introduced dried shrimp to South America and the Africans use them as a major, and sometimes essential, ingredient in the *vatapás*, the chicken and seafood stews, for which Bahia is justly famous. I find the quantities called for in many recipes (sometimes as much as a quarter of a pound) excessive but the amount can be adjusted without loss of ethnic flair. Most Bahian dishes, especially the rather complex *moquecas*, *vatapás* and *xinxins*, involve so many ingredients and are so beautifully orchestrated that single ingredients do not stand out. For many people the pungent, almost "ripe," aroma and flavor of dried shrimp are extremely appealing.

Spices, nuts, and seeds are also important to Bahian cooking, and gratitude is due the African heritage of the great women cooks. Adept with mortar and pestle, they still follow the time-honored custom of grinding garlic, peppers, and spices to a paste with salt before adding them to a dish. Nuts and seeds are also pounded and fresh ginger is frequently included. Today, the peanut-sauced stews of West Africa and the *vatapás* of Brazil are closely related.

Fresh coconut and coconut milk are essential components of the cooking along the tropical coasts of South America, Bahia included. These distinctive and versatile ingredients are used imaginatively in dishes ranging from soups to desserts and they are necessary to the great Bahian seafood and meat stews.

The cooking of Bahia might have developed into an interesting, but perhaps not particularly unusual, cuisine had it not been for the sugarcane plantations, with their slaves and Big Houses, and the particular life-styles that developed around them. The Portuguese established the first modern societies in tropical America and, in doing so, they succeeded where other Europeans had succumbed to the oppressiveness of the climate and geography. The Portuguese men quickly formed unions with both Indian and African women to produce a *mestizo* population more vigorous and better adapted to the tropical climate than any one of the originals.

According to Gilberto Freyre, who wrote a comprehensive and fascinating book called *The Masters and the Slaves*, the Portuguese colonizer differed in a number of ways from his Spanish and English counterpart. He had "no absolute ideas and no unyielding prejudices. He was least cruel in his relations with his slaves and he was inclined toward a voluptuous contact with exotic women."

The early food of the Big Houses, while it ostensibly satisfied the Portuguese masters, was actually nutritionally deficient, lacking in meats and vegetables and heavily laden with sweets and pastries. The slaves fared better. Although few luxuries were provided them, the larger quantities of corn, salt pork, and beans in their diets gave them strength to do hard physical labor and provided meals that were nutritionally more balanced than those enjoyed by the Portuguese.

It took the enterprising African women but a short time to achieve a place of their own in the New World. The Big House kitchens became their doman and, in their capacity as cooks, they preserved many of their own culinary traditions (which were as advanced as those of the Portuguese) and many of their own foods as well. They also became adept at transforming Indian cakes and confections from rather primitive fare into delicacies still enjoyed by Brazilians today. The great stewlike *moquecas* of Bahia are evolved African translations of Indian *pokekas*.

Brazil is an exuberant country with a population that includes fun-loving people who flock to the beaches, stay up late, and eat heartily. In Bahia, this national exuberance teams up with a primitive vitality derived from the multiracial heritage that permeates every aspect of life, especially the food. The mixing and blending, picking and choosing practiced by the African cooks has resulted in a truly unique cuisine and the status of these women cooks remains high today. There is an old saying: "*A mais preta a cozinheira, o melhor a comida,*" the blacker the cook, the better the food. It is still regarded as gospel.

mate gourd with oregano

The European Influence

The European influences on the cuisines of South America are far more diverse and complex than those of the native Indians and the imported Africans. The sixteenth century in Europe was a fascinating time that bridged the Renaissance and the Baroque. Explorations became truly global for the first time in 1522 when Juan Sebastian de Caro completed the voyage around the world begun by the Portuguese navigator, Ferdinand Magellan in 1519. It was not until 1580 that Sir Francis Drake circumnavigated the globe under the English flag but in the interim much traveling, exploring, conquering, and colonizing took place and the world changed dramatically.

Surprisingly soon after the Spanish and the Portuguese established their strongholds in the New World, shipments of food, plants, and animals arrived from the mother countries to supplement the newfound plenty. By the second generation a creole culture emerged, and with it a new cuisine. Based on local resources combined with imported foods, it made use of methods adopted from both and became the foundation of the South American cooking we know today. Diversity from country to country and from geographical region to region is combined with a rich variety from Europe.

Despite a common heritage on the Iberian peninsula, the Spanish and Portuguese went about the business of colonizing in very different ways. Both countries had only recently freed themselves from eight hundred years of Moorish domination during which the Portuguese had succumbed more than the Spanish had to the mysticism of Islam and the sensuous foods introduced by the conquerors from North Africa and the Middle East. And, in their colonial relationships, the Portuguese, although they took their Roman Catholic religion seriously, never, unlike the Spanish, became zealots.

From the beginning, the Portuguese colony in Brazil was based on agriculture. The primitive native Indian population proved negligible. The relationship between master and slave on the sugarcane plantations was generally less cruel than it was elsewhere and the Portuguese men were mixers who created a *mestizo* society within one generation. As a result, the family, rather than the church or the secular government became the stabilizing force in colonial Brazil.

210

The Spanish Conquest in other parts of South America, however, was just that—a conquest—and it almost always resulted in a clash of races, religions, and economic values. The Conquistadors, products as they were of a Spain dominated by the Inquisition, interpreted their religion as a charge to convert all heathens at all cost—a deadly serious mission in which the end almost always justified the means.

In agricultural areas, the *encomienda* system created an almost feudal society that emphasized and exaggerated class differences. The lordly colonizers styled their lives after those of Spanish grandees and were woefully out of touch with reality. They viewed all manual labor with disdain, were uninterested in technological improvements (choosing forced Indian labor instead), and allowed the power-seeking church to become the dominant institution in their creole society.

In 1570 they demonstrated their complete lack of understanding of the native population by establishing a branch of the Spanish Inquisition in Lima—their militant religious zeal carried to an extreme in a distant land. Throughout its history, the attitude of the Spanish colonialists was characterized by a narrow view and a defensive stance. At the same time, events in Europe made their colonial culture an anachronism in its own time.

Whatever their differences in establishing and managing a colonial society, food proved less of a problem than politics and both Spain and Portugal made valuable and lasting contributions to the cuisines of the new countries. The Portuguese also introduced a number of foods adopted from the Moorish tradition. Old Portuguese cookbooks still available in Brazil contain recipes for Moorish lamb, broth, fish, hen, and sausage. Even a brief sampling of Brazilian sweets establishes that the Moorish and Portuguese reliance on sugar and eggs successfully made the journey to the New World. The Moors get credit, too, for introducing oranges, lemons, and tangerines to Portugal and for passing along the art of preserving dried fruits. Colonial matrons took the preserving process with them to the colonies where they expanded it to include sweet confections of the exotic tropical fruits they encountered in their new homes. And *cuscuz*, a favorite dish in São Paulo today, cannot hide its North African heritage.

The so-called creole cuisines *are* today's South American cuisines. They consist of dishes, ways of cooking, and methods of using raw materials that have developed since the Conquest. Many European recipes necessarily made do with local ingredients at first although foods from Europe were soon available. Real creole cuisine is more likely to be available today in private homes or in remote areas. It is, however, generally easier to locate in Brazil than in the Spanish-speaking countries. *Feijoada*, the great Brazilian national dish, is served regularly in restaurants and the particular delights of the Bahian cuisine are available not only there but in other parts of the country as well.

Many of Brazil's rich sugar and egg desserts are too cloyingly sweet for most North American tastes, but their names are irresistible. The recipes for the popular cakes and cookies come from the Big Houses and from the nuns who lived in the early Portuguese convents. Who could refuse a slice of Hoping for a Husband Cake? Or a plate of Little Mother-in-Law Kisses? Or, perhaps, Kisses of the Farmer's Daughter? Dreams, Sighs, Gypsies, Embraces, Tinderboxes, and Maiden's Delights? Sociologists have noted an erotic quality to the names given to particular sweets by the cloistered nuns. Were Nun's Sighs, Heavenly Mana, Angel's Tidbits, and Nun's Bellies meant to please (or appease) male admirers in one of the few acceptable ways?

Soups and stews, the *sopas*, *caldos*, and *cocidos* of Spain and Portugal, almost at once became important in South America. They have been changed, sometimes much, sometimes little, by generations of cooks but many still represent their native regions with a humble accuracy. It was once a custom in wealthy Peruvian homes for a meat and vegetable stew to be brought to the table just after the first course. Untouched by the family and quickly taken away, it was presented to the master to assure him, in sight of his guests and family, that the servants for whom the dish was intended were eating well. This charming ritual is seldom performed today because the family, whatever their social standing, is quite likely to eat the stew themselves.

Portuguese colonists were accustomed to large quantities of seafood in their diets and in Brazil they discovered an even greater abundance and variety than they knew at home. Despite the generous supply of fresh fish and shrimp, however, they continued to rely on dried shrimp and dried salt cod, beloved staples that accompanied them wherever in the world they settled. The unwritten rules of the Portuguese export trade assured not only that dried salt cod and dried shrimp but also cheeses, sheep, olives, olive oil, almonds, and Port and Madeira wines were on their way to the new colony almost immediately and, of course, these imports gave a strong traditional boost to the local cooking. In the Spanish colonies, the situation was much the same; "necessities" from home arrived in the New World with amazing speed.

Climate and geography also proved important in shaping creole cuisines. Although much of South America is tropical, the continent is known for the wide ranging variety in climate and terrain. Tropical fruits, coconuts, and seafood are important in all the countries. The *ceviches* of Ecuador, Peru and Chile (each one claims it as its own) are among the great creole dishes. Particularly wonderful combinations of meat and fruit reflect not only the Moorish tradition but also the availability of local fruit.

When the Europeans arrived at the start of the sixteenth century, the only domesticated animals in South America were the highland llamas, alpacas, and vicuñas all of which were infrequently killed for food. The only other animal food of any consequence was the tiny guinea pig, another native of the Andes. When cattle, pigs, and sheep were introduced, the creoles again took up their meat eating habits but today, in many parts of South America, little meat is eaten. Good grazing land is often unavailable; for many people it is financially out of the question, and for others it simply is not an important part of their diet.

That, however, is not true in Argentina, Uruguay, and parts of Brazil, the lands of the *gaucho* whose colorful life-style is as obsolete today as that of the North American cowboy. In Argentina and Uruguay, beef is the preferred meat but lamb is popular for barbecues in Argentina and, in the Andean countries, is more available than beef. Brazil raises far more beef than it consumes and Argentina exports large quantities of canned corned beef.

Among the less affluent everywhere on the continent, dried beef is the major source of animal protein. *Carne sêca* or *charque*, as the dried meat is called, resembles beef jerky but is cured by a different process. Strips of meat are painted with a brine solution, dried in the sun, and painted again with the brine while drying. Lamb is sometimes prepared in the same way. Dried meats are an important ingredient in the Brazilian *feijoada* and are sometimes added to other long-cooking stewlike dishes as well.

Barbecues are taken seriously in South America where they are a delight. Simple restaurants called *parrilladas*, which serve charcoal grilled meats almost exclusively, are popular in all the meat-eating countries. A mixed grill in a South American restaurant or home, however, might make a North American wary: very little of the animal does not eventually arrive at the table.

The great *asados*, the legendary feasts of the *gauchos*, are largely a thing of the past except when they are staged for special celebrations. At an authentic *asado*, huge pieces of meat are roasted over an open fire. Whole sheep, goats, pigs, and lambs are split, impaled on metal rods, and placed at an angle over a very hot, but slow-burning wood fire. Beef is cut into large pieces, whole sides usually, and roasted in the same way. Sometimes these feasts include *carne con cuero*, meat roasted with the hide still on. Considered a delicacy, it requires special cooking skills and is especially appreciated by the meat-hungry Argentines.

Typical creole food is far more than a simple blend of the Spanish, Portuguese, and Indian traditions and foods. It is also *not* Spanish or Portuguese cooking per se. Since the first settlers arrived, other immigrants from Europe and the Far East have played their parts to help enrich the cuisines. The huge Brazilian city of São Paulo, the most populous on the continent, is home to more people from all over the world than is any other city in South America. It includes one of the largest Japanese communities outside the Orient as well as Germans and Italians who emigrated to Brazil in large numbers. In Rio de Janeiro, the Portuguese influence is still the most widely felt. Argentina and Uruguay are both home to significant Italian and German populations and to lesser ones from England, Ireland, and Switzerland.

Although immigrants are generally well-integrated, ethnic pockets are found all over South America. The La Boca section of Buenos Aires is as colorful a Little Italy—with food to match—as exists anywhere. In landlocked Paraguay, many citizens are of Italian extraction, although there most of the cooking traditions come from the Spanish or the Guarani Indians. To the Germans goes credit for much of the continent's good cheese and beer. Most South American countries make excellent cheeses, among them seldom-exported local specialties and good versions of many Old World varieties.

As we all become more international in our eating habits and as foods from south of the border become more available to us, the differences today between the cuisines of North and South America are often those of cooking method and final preparation rather than of specific ingredients. The great international exchange of foodstuffs and culinary ideas that began in the sixteenth century is still going on. How fortunate we are to participate.

Bibliography

Andrade, Margarette de. *Brazilian Cookery, Traditional and Modern*. Rio de Janeiro: Livro Eldorado, 1982.

André-Engle, Frederick. *An Ancient World Preserved, Relics and Records of Prehistory in the Andes*. Translated by Rachel Kendall Gordon. New York: Crown, 1976.

Andrews, Jean. *Peppers, The Domesticated Capsicums*. Austin, Texas: University of Texas Press, 1984.

Arciniegas, Germán. *Latin America: A Cultural History*. Translated by Joan MacLean. New York: Knopf, 1968.

Bailey, Adrian. *Cook's Ingredients*. New York: William Morrow, 1980.

Beck, Bruce. *Produce*. New York: Friendly Press, 1984.

Brenuil. *Peruvian Dishes, Platos Peruvanos*. Lima, Peru: A.B.C. S.A. 1980.

Brown, Cora, Rose Brown, and Robert Brown. *South American Cookbook, Including Central America, Mexico and the West Indies*. New York: Doubleday, Doran, 1939; New York: Dover, 1979.

Cost, Bruce. *Ginger East to West; Revised and Expanded*. Reading, MA: Addison-Wesley, 1989.

Crosby, Alfred W., Jr. *The Columbian Exchange, Biological and Cultural Consequences of 1492*. Westport, Conn.: Greenwood, 1972.

Farb, Peter, and George Armelagos. *Consuming Passions, The Anthropology of Eating*. Boston, Mass.: Houghton, Mifflin, 1980.

Freyre, Gilberto. *The Masters and the Slaves*. Translated by Samuel Putnam. New York: Knopf, 1946.

Gordon, Lesley. *A Country Herbal*. Exeter, England: Webb and Bower, 1980.

Gorenstein, Shirley, Richard G. Forbes, Paul Tolstoy, and Edward P. Lanning. *Prehispanic America*. New York: St. Martin's, 1974.

Hardy, Jorge E. *Pre-Columbian Cities*. New York: Walker, 1973.

Hemming, John. *The Conquest of the Incas*. New York: Harcourt Brace Jovanovich, 1970.

Hellman, Howard, and Dana Shilling. *The Book of World Cuisines*. England: Penguin, 1979.

Jones, Evan. *American Food, The Gastronomic Story*. New York: Random House, 1981.

215

Leonard, Jonathan Norton. *Latin American Cooking*. New York: Time-Life Books, 1968, 1979.

Marcus, George, and Nancy Marcus. *Forbidden Fruits and Forgotten Vegetables*. New York: St. Martin's, 1982.

Meisch, Lynn. *A Traveler's Guide To El Dorado and the Inca Empire*. New York: Viking Penguin, 1984.

Ortiz, Elisabeth Lambert. *The Book of Latin American Cooking*. New York: Vintage, 1980.

Picon-Salas, Mariano. *A Cultural History of Spanish America From Conquest to Independence*. Berkeley: University of California Press, 1962.

Ritchie, Carson I. A. *Food in Civilization, How Food Has Been Affected by Human Tastes*. New York, Toronto: Beaufort, 1981.

Root, Waverly. *Food*. New York: Simon and Schuster, 1980.

Seward, Julian H., and Louis C. Faron. *Native Peoples of South America*. New York: McGraw-Hill, 1959.

Tannahill, Reay. *Food in History*. New York: Stein and Day, 1973.

Tschiffely, A. F. *Southern Cross to Pole Star*. New York: Simon and Schuster, 1933; Los Angeles: J. P. Tarcher, 1933.

Tume, Lynelle. *Latin American Cooking*. Printing, Ltd., Dee Why West, Australia: Paul Hamlyn, 1979; Secaucus, N.J.: Chartwell, n.d.

Zurek, Teresita Roman de, Amparo Roman de Velez, and Olga Roman Velez. *Cartagena de indias en la olla, cocina tipica Colombiana e internacional*. Cartagena, Colombia: Decimaquinta Edicion, 1981.

Index